THE OTHER TUDOR PRINCESS

THE OTHER TUDOR PRINCESS

MARGARET DOUGLAS, HENRY VIII's NIECE

MARY McGRIGOR

To my darling daughters, Lorna and Kirsty.

First published 2015

The History Press
The Mill, Brimscombe Port
Stroud, Gloucestershire, GL5 2QG
www.thehistorypress.co.uk

British Library Cataloguing in Publication Data.
A catalogue record for this book is available from the British Library.

ISBN 978 0 7509 6123 3

Typesetting and origination by The History Press
Printed in Europe

CONTENTS

ACKNOWLEDGEMENTS

My deepest thanks to all those who have helped me with the book, including: Roy Summers for his beautiful photographs of the Scottish castles known to Lady Margaret in her day; Michael and Charlotte Wemyss; my godson, Adrian Gibbs, Deputy CEO at the Bridgeman Art Library Ltd; Elizabeth L. Taylor, Rights and Images Officer at the National Portrait Gallery; Ryan Clee, Photography and Licensing Assistant at the National Galleries of Scotland and Manju Nair, Finance Assistant of the gallery. Thanks also to Agata Rutkowska, Picture Library Assistant, Royal Collection Trust; Brigadier Henry Wilson; Sophie Bradshaw, General History Publisher, and Juanita Zoë Hall, Managing Editor, at The History Press. I am indepted to Archie Mackenzie for his valuable advice.

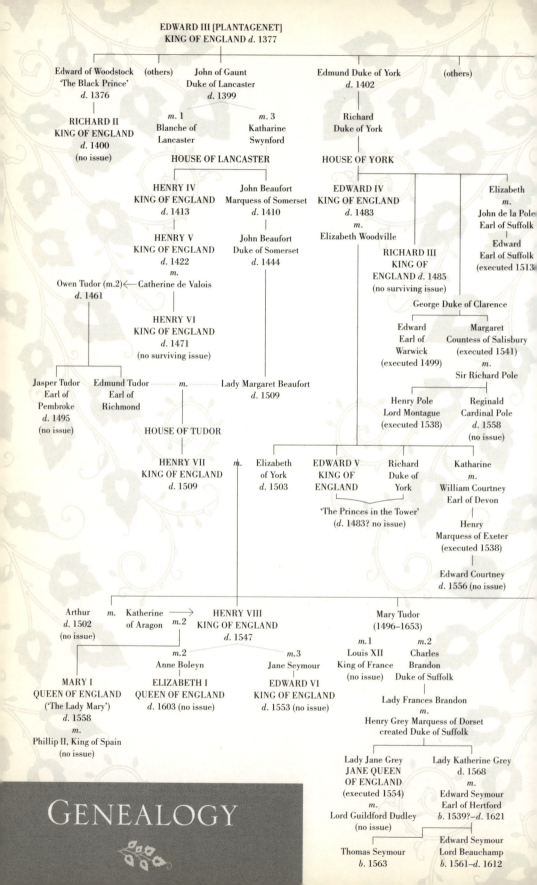

EDWARD III [PLANTAGENET]
KING OF ENGLAND *d.* 1377

Edward of Woodstock
'The Black Prince'
d. 1376

(others)

John of Gaunt
Duke of Lancaster
d. 1399

Edmund Duke of York
d. 1402

(others)

RICHARD II
KING OF ENGLAND
d. 1400
(no issue)

m. 1
Blanche of
Lancaster

m. 3
Katharine
Swynford

Richard
Duke of York

HOUSE OF LANCASTER

HOUSE OF YORK

HENRY IV
KING OF ENGLAND
d. 1413

John Beaufort
Marquess of Somerset
d. 1410

EDWARD IV
KING OF ENGLAND
d. 1483
m.
Elizabeth Woodville

Elizabeth
m.
John de la Pole
Earl of Suffolk

HENRY V
KING OF ENGLAND
d. 1422
m.

John Beaufort
Duke of Somerset
d. 1444

RICHARD III
KING OF
ENGLAND *d.* 1485
(no surviving issue)

Edward
Earl of Suffolk
(executed 1513)

Owen Tudor (m.2) ← Catherine de Valois
d. 1461

George Duke of Clarence

HENRY VI
KING OF ENGLAND
d. 1471
(no surviving issue)

Edward
Earl of
Warwick
(executed 1499)

Margaret
Countess of Salisbury
(executed 1541)
m.
Sir Richard Pole

Jasper Tudor
Earl of
Pembroke
d. 1495
(no issue)

Edmund Tudor
Earl of
Richmond

m.

Lady Margaret Beaufort
d. 1509

Henry Pole
Lord Montague
(executed 1538)

Reginald
Cardinal Pole
d. 1558
(no issue)

HOUSE OF TUDOR

HENRY VII
KING OF ENGLAND
d. 1509

m.

Elizabeth
of York
d. 1503

EDWARD V
KING OF
ENGLAND

Richard
Duke of
York

Katharine
m.
William Courtney
Earl of Devon

'The Princes in the Tower'
(*d.* 1483? no issue)

Henry
Marquess of Exeter
(executed 1538)

Edward Courtney
d. 1556 (no issue)

Arthur
d. 1502
(no issue)

m.

Katherine
of Aragon
*m.*2

HENRY VIII
KING OF ENGLAND
d. 1547

Mary Tudor
(1496–1653)

*m.*1
Louis XII
King of France
(no issue)

*m.*2
Charles
Brandon
Duke of Suffolk

*m.*2
Anne Boleyn

*m.*3
Jane Seymour

MARY I
QUEEN OF ENGLAND
('The Lady Mary')
d. 1558
m.
Phillip II, King of Spain
(no issue)

ELIZABETH I
QUEEN OF ENGLAND
d. 1603 (no issue)

EDWARD VI
KING OF ENGLAND
d. 1553 (no issue)

Lady Frances Brandon
m.
Henry Grey Marquess of Dorset
created Duke of Suffolk

Lady Jane Grey
JANE QUEEN
OF ENGLAND
(executed 1554)
m.
Lord Guildford Dudley
(no issue)

Lady Katherine Grey
d. 1568
m.
Edward Seymour
Earl of Hertford
b. 1539?–*d.* 1621

Thomas Seymour
b. 1563

Edward Seymour
Lord Beauchamp
b. 1561–*d.* 1612

GENEALOGY

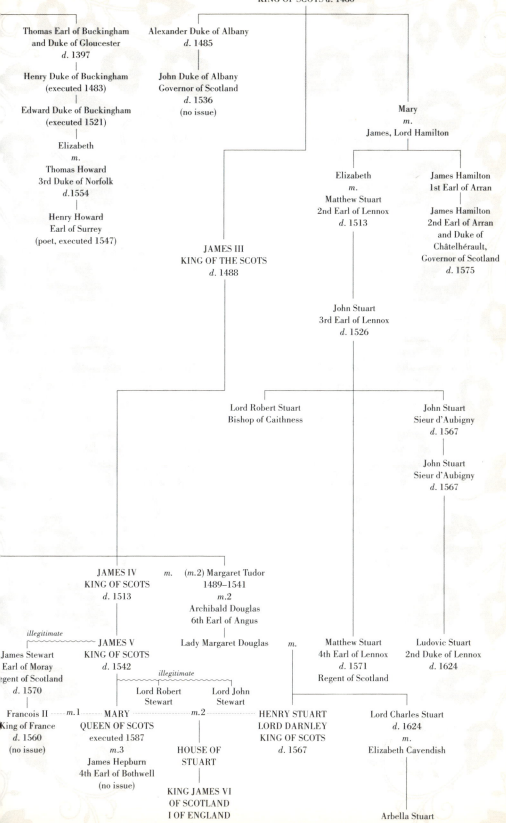

JAMES II [STEWART]
KING OF SCOTS d. 1460

Thomas Earl of Buckingham
and Duke of Gloucester
d. 1397

Henry Duke of Buckingham
(executed 1483)

Edward Duke of Buckingham
(executed 1521)

Elizabeth
m.
Thomas Howard
3rd Duke of Norfolk
d.1554

Henry Howard
Earl of Surrey
(poet, executed 1547)

Alexander Duke of Albany
d. 1485

John Duke of Albany
Governor of Scotland
d. 1536
(no issue)

Mary
m.
James, Lord Hamilton

Elizabeth
m.
Matthew Stuart
2nd Earl of Lennox
d. 1513

James Hamilton
1st Earl of Arran

James Hamilton
2nd Earl of Arran
and Duke of
Châtelhérault,
Governor of Scotland
d. 1575

JAMES III
KING OF THE SCOTS
d. 1488

John Stuart
3rd Earl of Lennox
d. 1526

Lord Robert Stuart
Bishop of Caithness

John Stuart
Sieur d'Aubigny
d. 1567

John Stuart
Sieur d'Aubigny
d. 1567

JAMES IV   m.   (m.2) Margaret Tudor
KING OF SCOTS   1489–1541
d. 1513   m.2
                          Archibald Douglas
                          6th Earl of Angus

illegitimate
JAMES V   Lady Margaret Douglas   m.
KING OF SCOTS
James Stewart   d. 1542
Earl of Moray
egent of Scotland   illegitimate
d. 1570
                   Lord Robert   Lord John
                   Stewart   Stewart

Matthew Stuart
4th Earl of Lennox
d. 1571
Regent of Scotland

Ludovic Stuart
2nd Duke of Lennox
d. 1624

Francois II   m.1   MARY   m.2   HENRY STUART   Lord Charles Stuart
King of France   QUEEN OF SCOTS   LORD DARNLEY   d. 1624
d. 1560   executed 1587   KING OF SCOTS   m.
(no issue)   m.3   d. 1567   Elizabeth Cavendish
                    James Hepburn   HOUSE OF
                    4th Earl of Bothwell STUART
                    (no issue)
                                    KING JAMES VI
                                    OF SCOTLAND
                                    I OF ENGLAND   Arbella Stuart

THE BEGINNING

Late one evening in August 1515, darkness was falling on Linlithgow Palace, shading the sides of the courtyard from the naked eye. Within it a small group was gathered, a party of well-armed men and several women. One of the women was obviously with child, evident despite the cloak she wore. The party moved quietly from the courtyard barely visible in the deepening dusk. Outside horses were waiting, one with a pillion behind the saddle onto which the pregnant woman was lifted. A tall young man stood beside her as she was helped from the ground, then quickly mounted himself to lead the party from the castle. The sentries stood aside to let him pass, well briefed on what was about to happen.

Riding hard, they had covered a scant 3 miles towards the City of Edinburgh when the Lord Chamberlain, Lord Home, met them with a party Queen Margaret later described as 'hardy, well-striking fellows'. The men were to escort her to her husband, the Earl of Angus' castle of Tantallon, who was waiting for her on the east coast of Scotland, near what was then the ferry port of North Berwick.

Twenty-six-year-old Margaret, the daughter of Henry VII of England, had married nineteen-year-old Angus just a year after her first husband, King James IV, had died in the dreadful scrimmage of Flodden. The marriage in itself had been one reason why the leaders of the Scottish nobility had summoned John, Duke of Albany, to come to Scotland as regent.

John was the son of Alexander, brother of James III, who had become domiciled in France after his exile from Scotland. When Alexander was killed in an accident, his French wife Anne de la Tour d'Auvergne raised their only child alone. More French than Scottish, John was nonetheless heir to the throne of Scotland after James IV's two sons.

Albany, as he was always entitled, landed at Dumbarton in May 1515. He was at first on good terms with Margaret but held the opinion that her husband was an incompetent youth. Having immured herself with the two little princes of her previous marriage, Margaret surrendered them to the care of Albany before publicly announcing that she was 'taking her chamber' and entering confinement until the birth of her child by Angus was born.

The subterfuge had been clever. Playing on the fact that she was known to have suffered greatly during the births of her previous children, she had managed to convince her attendants that she was now so ill that Angus had to be summoned to her side. It was he who had asked Lord Home to help them, knowing as he did that Albany, having accused Home of being responsible for the death of James IV at Flodden, was now an avowed enemy.

Escorted by Lord Home and his men, Margaret and Angus reached Tantallon, the red sandstone fortress of the Red Douglasses, dominating the cliffs above the North Sea opposite the Bass Rock.

There they waited with ever increasing impatience for a rider bringing a summons from King Henry VIII, Margaret's brother, to come to his court in England.

The summons never came. Home, seizing the chance to raid some of Albany's property in the Queen's name, was declared an outlaw. He too fled to Tantallon, joining Margaret and Angus until they all fled for his own land on 23 September. There, in Coldstream Nunnery, Home's mother came to Margaret's aid for she was now genuinely exhausted and seriously ill.

At last King Henry's invitation arrived. A message was sent to Lord Dacre who at once sent an escort to take Margaret across the Border to his family home of Morpeth Castle. Fires were lit and comforts of every kind prepared by members of the household who were told of her imminent arrival. The distance to Morpeth was some 50 miles. Margaret was carried in a litter, which although most carefully handled, jolted her arthritic hip. Towards the end of their journey, when they were only 14 miles from the town of Rothbury, Margaret felt a familiar pain. Her bearers, hearing her cry out that she could go no farther, turned to their mounted escort for advice. It was plain they could not reach Morpeth, another 20 miles on from Rothbury. In such a state of emergency there was only one alternative: Lord Dacre owned the outlying fortress of Harbottle, a medieval castle strategically built on a mound overlooking the River Coquet. A stark stone building, used primarily as a prison, it had long needed repair. The roof leaked above walls running with damp. It was certainly no place for any woman, particularly one of royal blood, to give birth.

But it was at least shelter from the wind and the driving rain. In the present situation there was no alternative other than to carry Margaret, now shrieking in agony, into the cold bare tower.

1

The Refugee

'Women! A plague to mankind and the royal ones the worst of the lot.' Thomas, Lord Dacre, Warden of the Marches on the English side and terror of all those in his thrall, was driven to desperation by the screaming within his castle walls. Queen Margaret was bad enough. The agony of her long labour combined with the pain in her hip had kept her yelling for three days or more; now, on top of Margaret's screams, the furious bawling of a hungry infant was driving him out of his mind.

'For God's sake find a wet-nurse,' he roared at his terrified servants, one of whom had the temerity to remind him that the commotion upstairs in the draughty, mouse-infested castle with its leaking roof, was partly his own fault. On the fugitive queen's arrival, he had forbidden her ladies to come within its walls.

Lord Dacre was at his wits' end, faced with an unexpected emergency such as he had never met before. War had just broken out again between England and Scotland and now, in early October, taking advantage of the ensuing confusion, rustlers were lifting cattle, fat on summer grass. He had just come in from a hard day's riding trying to track them down, and had been looking forward to an evening's rest before the fire in his castle of Morpeth when a man on a horse, streaked with sweat from hard galloping, had appeared with the news that the Queen of Scots had arrived at the Border fort of Harbottle. Obviously in labour, she seemed on the point of death.

She had remained thus for forty-eight hours until, to the intense relief of every man and woman within the castle, she had given birth to an infant, which (with hair the colour of the Red Douglasses) had proved to be a girl. Named after her mother, she had been baptised the very next day, the usual custom at a time when infant mortality was so great as to be expected rather than merely feared. Her godfather was Cardinal Wolsey, for whom one of the men in the castle had stood proxy.

Two days later, on 10 October, Queen Margaret, still extremely weak, had dictated a letter to the Duke of Albany saying that 'she had been forced, for fear and danger of her life, to depart from Scotland to the realm of England'. [1]

Lord Dacre was afterwards accused of failing to report the birth of his niece to Henry VIII; had he done so, the messenger would surely have been either killed or captured as soon as the portcullis was raised. Raiding parties from just over the border in Scotland were seen by the sentries from the battlements, and rumours had already reached the castle that the Regent Albany, who had seized all the queen's clothes and jewellery as well as anything worth lifting from her husband's castle of Tantallon, was advancing on Harbottle with 40,000 men.

As sentries reported that men on horseback could be seen coming from the north, mounting to the battlements, Lord Dacre recognised to his great relief, the standard of the queen's husband, the Earl of Angus, riding at the head of them. Beside him was Lord Home, together with several other so-called 'rebel lords'.

Despite having little on which to feed them after living in a virtual state of siege, Lord Dacre allowed them to enter the fortress. Once within its walls, they signed a covenant binding them to free Margaret's two little sons, James V and his brother Alexander Duke of Ross, from the regent, whose power would then be given to the queen. The signatures of her husband Angus, Earl of Douglas; the Earl of Arran, head of the house of Hamilton; and Lord Hume, are all appended to this document, called a bond, which is dated 15 October 1515. [2]

Despite the discomfort of Harbottle, where the wind found its way through every crack in the uncovered walls, Queen Margaret was too ill to travel until the beginning of November. Then with a strong escort, she moved on to the Castle of Morpeth, Lord Dacre's family home.

No greater contrast could be found than that between the castles of Harbottle, comfortless in every aspect, and Morpeth. The latter fortress, although built a mere hundred years later than the former, on a hill overlooking the River Wansbeck, was nonetheless as luxurious as any building of its day. A curtain wall contained the gatehouse beyond which, in the centre of the courtyard, rose the Great Tower. The rooms, so unlike the damp cold chambers of Harbottle, were hung with tapestries and warmed with fires. In the dining hall on the first floor, the table gleamed with silverware, which sparkled in the light thrown by candles from sconces on the walls.

Revelling in the newfound comfort, Margaret was further overjoyed by presents of lengths of velvet and cloth of gold sent by her brother Henry with an envoy, Sir Christopher Gargrave. Delighted, she summoned seamstresses: Margaret was inordinately fond of new gowns. The gifts included baby clothes, thoughtfully provided by Queen Catherine of Aragon, now pregnant with what she and the king hoped most fervently would prove to be a son.

The winter went by at Morpeth as Queen Margaret gradually regained her strength. In February news came from England that Queen Catherine had borne a daughter, so far her one surviving child.

Slowly the days lengthened, and the roads, in a spell of dry weather, became open to travel; at the beginning of April a cavalcade from England arrived. This time it included William Blackwall, a gentleman of the bedchamber and the clerk of the King's Spicery. He came with silver vessels for use on her journey. There were drinking cups and probably some pots and a kettle that could be heated on a wood or charcoal fire. In addition, Queen Catherine sent her equerry, Sir Thomas Parr, with her own favourite white pony, carrying a specially padded pillion on which her sister-in-law, riding behind a groom, would have almost as much comfort as had she been carried in a litter. Her baby Margaret, together with her nurse, travelled in the latter way.

When preparations for the journey were complete, Angus, whom King Henry had specifically included in his sister's invitation to his court, suddenly disappeared to Scotland. He claimed that he had gone to make his peace with the regent, but most people knew, some tittering behind their hands, that he was returning to his mistress, Janet Stewart, daughter of the Laird of Traquair.

2

'MY NIECE MARGET'

Smothering her anger at his desertion (she is claimed never to have forgiven him), Queen Margaret made her journey to London in slow stages. Mortified as she was by her husband's behaviour, it was at least some consolation that at each and all of her resting places she found herself royally received. She is known to have stopped at Stony Stratford in North Buckinghamshire, the ancient market town where the ford of the Roman road of Watling Street crosses the Great Ouse. From there, on 27 April, she wrote to her brother, sending the letter with a fast rider to warn him of her approach.

Two days later she reached Enfield, almost within sight of London. Here she stayed in Enfield Palace, the palatial Middlesex home of Sir William Lovell, speaker of the House of Commons and Lord Treasurer of the Household under Cardinal Wolsey's administration. Her brother King Henry, himself a frequent visitor, drawn by the luxury of the house as well as the political importance of Lovell, had requested him to receive his sister for a visit of four days.

Queen Margaret reached Tottenham Cross on 3 May, which by the Gregorian calendar would have been 12 May, on a reputedly beautiful morning. This was then the station to which all processions from the north gates in London and elsewhere in the British Isles converged. There, as was pre-arranged, she waited until a gorgeous concord appeared to the sound of trumpets and a great clattering of horses' hooves.

Preceded only by his standard bearer, the flag with the arms of England unfurling in the breeze against the sky, Henry headed the procession. Distinguished by his height and his spectacular apparel (a velvet cloak falling from his shoulders above the intricately worked steel breastplate he always wore for safety, even on such occasions), Henry was still the handsome prince on that day of his reunion with his eldest sister. He would, however, have been stouter than when she had last seen him, as chroniclers on his succession so rapturously described.

Having embraced her, his first words to Margaret were reputedly, 'Where is my Lord Angus?' Whereupon, told of his sudden, unexplained disappearance, he slapped his thigh exclaiming, 'Done like a Scot!'

Instantly, his anger vanished as his sister held out the baby, by now six months old. Raising her high in his arms, he called her his little Marget, his special name for her which he would always continue to use.

Queen Margaret rode into the city of London on a pillion behind Sir Thomas Parr, while behind, in the following procession, came her baby in the horse litter, held securely by her nurse. It was six in the evening before they reached Baynard's Castle, made ready for her by her brother. This was the mansion built on land reclaimed from the Thames, on a site just east of what is now Blackfriar's Station. It was reconstructed as a royal palace by Henry and Margaret's grandfather, Henry VII, and had been given to Catherine of Aragon. However, despite the splendour of her surroundings, Margaret was eager to leave. Within days she was boarding a barge from the wharf that took her, with her attendants and tiny daughter, down the Thames to Greenwich Palace.

Rebuilt by her father, Henry VII, using no less than 600,000 bricks fired by his own brickmakers in Greenwich, this was now not only the largest but also the most modern palace in Europe. It was here only three months earlier on 18 February that the little Princess Mary, Margaret's niece and her brother's only surviving child, had been born.

His sister Margaret and her baby daughter were warmly welcomed by Queen Catherine, now grown stout and matronly but still possessing a soft voice with a charming Spanish inflection. Catherine cried out with delight at sight of little Margaret, now crowned with the small tight curls of glorious red-gold hair so indicative of her Tudor descent. Catherine's own daughter, Mary, five months younger than Margaret, was small in comparison and as dark as she was fair. The two infants shared a nursery, thus beginning, although neither was aware of it at the time, a friendship which would last throughout their lives.

In the palace was yet another infant, this time a little boy named Henry, born only on 11 March. He was the son of Henry's youngest and favourite sister, the Princess Mary; despite his fondness for Mary, he had used her as a political pawn, sending her to France to marry Louis XII, a man thirty-four years older than herself. Before leaving, however, she had made her brother promise that in the event of her husband's death (which in fact happened after only eighty-two days, supposedly after consummating his marriage with his young bride) she might marry whom she chose. Subsequently, while still in France, she had secretly married Charles Brandon, Duke of Suffolk with whom, although he was again much older than herself, she had long been in love. Henry, who in fact had sent Suffolk to fetch her, although officially protesting, had forgiven them; a formal marriage ceremony had taken place in Greenwich Palace only a few days before her elder sister, Margaret, the former Queen of Scotland, had arrived.

Princess Mary, renowned both for her sweet face and equally lovable temper – she had nursed the French king devotedly during their brief marriage – greatly loved children. She is known to have been particularly fond of her little niece Margaret, to whom later she was to be almost a second mother. Now, although the Duchess of Suffolk, she was still known as the French Queen.

Evidence of the presence of King Henry's wife and his two sisters being together at Greenwich in May 1516 is found in the illustration on the front page of one of his music books, kept in the Harleian Collection. Below the arms of England are shown the badges of Henry VIII and Catherine of Aragon, the rose and the pomegranate, while opposite them are the daisy, called a marguerite, and a marigold denoting Mary.

Henry himself played with the children, tossing his little 'Marget' in the air. Otherwise he was occupied in arranging entertainments including a tournament in his sister Margaret's honour, in which he played a leading part, knocking over a burly knight called Sir William Kingston together with his horse!

Queen Margaret, meanwhile, although estranged from him, was still corresponding with her husband, Angus, urging him to do everything possible to help the English army to cause destruction on the Scottish Borders. Lord Dacre asked Cardinal Wolsey to get what information he could from her to aid him in a scheme to overthrow the regent, while she is claimed to have given secret information about Scotland to the English Council. Albany himself, having threatened to visit Henry's court, thought better of it. However, he did return the large collection of Margaret's jewels and court dresses (which had been taken from Tantallon Castle) with the Master of Graystock College, whom Dacre allowed to cross the Border.

During the season of Advent, Queen Margaret was moved to Scotland Yard – so called because kings of Scotland had once stayed there – within a court below Charing Cross. Later she went to Windsor Castle, before returning to Baynard's Castle, now stacked with presents from Henry (jewels, plate, tapestry and horses) which had to be taken back to Scotland.

Soon afterwards her brother urged her return. It was possible he was exasperated by her constant demands for money, yet Henry VIII was also famously devoid of scruples in using members of his family for political reasons. Word had reached England that the Regent Albany, due to his wife's illness, was about to return to France; Henry realised an opportunity to use Margaret as a diplomat – the widow of national hero James IV and revered for his sake if not her own – to effect a unity with England and end the ruination of continued war.

In the spring of 1517 she began her journey northwards, stopping for a time in York. Then she moved on to stay once again with Lord Dacre at Morpeth. Here she waited until news came that the Duke of Albany, hastening to return to France where his wife was dying, had sailed on 7 June. Travelling farther north to the border, the queen was met at Berwick by her husband, the Earl of Angus. The earl escorted her and their little daughter, now eighteen months old, to the palace of Holyrood below Edinburgh Castle, no longer in hostile hands.

3

WILD AS A
TANTALLON HAWK

Reaching Edinburgh, Queen Margaret immediately demanded to see her son James V, now a boy of nearly six. But he was rushed off to Craigmillar Castle at once on the excuse that Margaret or one of her attendants might be carrying the dreaded plague, or sweating sickness, which was rampant in England. At Craigmillar she was eventually allowed to see him but only for short amounts of time.

Writing to her brother King Henry, she reported her son to be in good health while taking the opportunity to suggest to him that he should seize the goods of merchants trading by ship with England to reimburse the income of her estates, which she claimed she had not received. It would seem that in her first infatuation she had made over the life-interest of the royal estates in Ettrick – part of her settlement at the time of her marriage to King James – to Angus.

Now, however, they were at loggerheads: their furious quarrels culminating in abduction when Angus seized their small daughter who was then only 3 years old. He took her to his castle at Tantallon, that massive rose-coloured fortress towering above the estuary of the Firth of Forth, defiant of bombardment, a landmark from afar against the sky.

For little Margaret, Tantallon was a haven. In his castle, mainly used as a barracks, her father found Douglas ladies to look after her. Amongst them were the wives of his brother George and his cousin Archibald. These chatelaines took care of the little girl, robbed of the mother who, unbeknown to her at the time, she would never see again.

It was from these Douglas women, proud as they were of their heritage, that she heard the story of the castle and the men who had made it one of the greatest bastions of the time.

William, the 1st Earl of Douglas, had been the founder in about 1350 almost 120 years before. He had chosen an almost impenetrable site above cliffs that only a madman would attempt to climb. Making certain of its safety, he had surrounded his castle with a massive curtain wall, 50ft high. Towers at each end of the rectangle were pierced with arrow slits through which archers could train their arrows on approaching foes from all directions. Finally, for extra security, a deep ditch had been dug to surround the walls.

William had taken no chances, carefully weighing up every eventuality that might possibly occur. Foremost, and most obvious, had been that of prolonged siege. Before even finding an architect, he had summoned a water diviner who, with a forked twig of hazel, had pinpointed the existence of a spring. Once water had been located and reached by drilling through the rock, a well in the courtyard had been surrounded by a stone wall.

It was Earl William who, having ambushed and killed his godfather, also named William Douglas, had tyrannised the Borders. The 3rd Earl, known for his ferocity as Archibald the Grim, had been followed by the heroic 'Black Douglas', famously hacked to pieces by the Saracens while carrying the heart of Bruce on a crusade to Spain.

Then had come the dreadful story of the 'Black Dinner'. The young King James II, only 10 years old at the time, had been greatly excited when the 14-year-old William Douglas and his brother David – to him men of the world – had come to dine at Edinburgh Castle. The little king, sitting at the head of the table spanning the length of the great hall, had grown sleepy, dazed by the effects of red wine, the heat from the fire and the clamour of voices. He had not understood the significance when, just as the dinner was ending, the head of a black bull, a portent of death, was carried in by the Chancellor, Sir William Crichton, and laid before the Douglas boys. He had cried out terrified as the brothers were hauled from the room. His pleas to spare them had gone unheeded: after being given a mock trial, they were executed on the castle hill.

Their great uncle, avaricious for their land and titles, had been their killer. Known as James the Gross for his bloated size, he was the 7th Earl. Meanwhile James II, dubbed 'Fiery Face' for a birthmark that matched his temper, had nursed his hatred of the Douglasses, whose power threatened his own. James the Gross had been succeeded by his son William on whom the king had wrought revenge. Summoned to Stirling under a safe conduct, William had been warmly received. A banquet had followed at which both had heavily imbibed. Then, drawing him into an alcove, James had asked William to forgo his alliance with the Earls of Crawford and Ross. William, haughty in his cups, had refused and James, uncontrolled in fury, had stabbed him above his steel corselet with a dagger in the throat. He had not actually killed him, but the Master of Gray, one of his bodyguards, had the murder of a nephew to avenge and had finished him off with an axe.

The murdered William's brother James, the 9th Earl, had been exiled and forfeited after King James' cannons had destroyed his castle's walls. The last of the Black Douglass earls, his lands and titles had then devolved upon George Douglas, 4th Earl of Angus.

It was George's son, Archibald, born in Tantallon in 1449, who was notorious for hanging James III's favourites over the Bridge of Lauder and was famously known thereafter as 'Bell the Cat'.

Archibald's son George (Margaret's grandfather) had been killed in the melee at the Battle of Flodden, thus Margaret's father, the red-haired Archibald, had become the 6th Earl as a very young man.

During the daytime, the castle echoed with noise as the men of the garrison and the servants tramped up and down the stone stairs. The family, as was then normal, dined in the great hall at about midday, but when Angus himself was absent, his little daughter, with her aunts in attendance, most likely kept to their apartments in the first floor of the main tower.

At night the sounds abated as the occupants settled down to sleep, the family in the upstairs bedrooms, the rest of the household on the floor by the fire of the great hall and elsewhere throughout the house. Upstairs, in the quiet of the night, the little girl, lying in one of the few beds, snuggled under a down filled quilt and listened to the cries of sea birds above waves crashing on the rocks.

But sometimes there were other sounds frightening and dreadful to hear. Deep in the foundations of the castle, buried into the cliff, prisoners in the dungeon groaned and screamed for help. Some of them, so the legend runs, were cast adrift on rafts and left to the mercy of the tides, which took a few to the Bass, where sometimes monks dragged them on to land. Others were simply carried to their deaths at sea.

Standing in the courtyard today it is hard to imagine what life in Tantallon Castle must have been like nearly 500 years ago for a little girl of 3.

It would be nice to think of her playing, like so many other children then and now, on the sands near the rock formation called St Baldred's Boat. However, it is more probable that because of the threat of abduction by the Regent Albany's and her mother's men, she was kept within the safety of the castle; she was probably allowed, in fine weather, to play in the courtyard or under surveillance close by.

In the spring and summer months, there was always the diversion of the colony of gannets, diving into the sea like arrows from their sanctuary on the Bass Rock. Later, when the chicks were hatched, men climbed down the rock, held by ropes from above, to collect the fledglings, which when smoked were a much-prized delicacy to eat.

Before John Duke of Albany left Scotland in May 1517, a commission of regency had been given to a confederacy consisting of the Archbishops of Glasgow and St Andrews; the earls of Angus, Huntly, Arran and Argyll; and Seigneur Antoine d'Arces, de la Bastie, Albany's Scottish Agent. There were French garrisons in the castles of Dunbar, Dumbarton and Inchgarvie, the island in the Forth from where the Queen's Ferry was guarded. Hardly had Albany set sail before de la Bastie was murdered in a fracas with the Homes. Arran, a son of James III's sister Mary who had married Lord Hamilton, a first cousin of the regent, then took over as head of the council, supported by Argyll, Huntly and James Beaton, Archbishop of Glasgow. However, this alliance was overruled by Angus, who, seeing the chance to win control, joined forces with the Homes and other dissident Borderers. With them, apparently to the joy of the populace, he drove the Hamiltons out of Edinburgh.

So complete was his predominance that in March 1520 Arran openly declared that 'he sould nocht cum within the toun quhill my Lord Chancelor [Beaton] maid ane finall concord betuix him and the nychbouris thairof.'[1]

This was the incident known thereafter as 'Cleanse the Causeway'. So fraught was the situation that in the following October it was decreed that the Provost of Edinburgh must be neither a Douglas nor a Hamilton and should always be accompanied by four stout halberdiers. Further to this it was suggested that to heal the rift between the families Angus' little daughter Margaret should marry Arran's son.

Margaret, probably not even told of this marriage brokerage, was still at Tantallon when on 19 November 1521 Albany returned from France. Coming ashore in the Gareloch, he rode to Linlithgow where – to what must have been to his and most people's great surprise – he was warmly welcomed by Queen Margaret. Brazenly, they rode together at the head of a procession from Linlithgow to Edinburgh, displaying rather more than friendship, or so King Henry was told.

Soon tongues were wagging as they began an adulterous affair; this was all the more scandalous because while the queen was known to be estranged from her husband, Albany was still married to his ailing wife, his first cousin Anne de la Tour d'Auvergne, daughter of his mother's brother, who had given her his sister's name.

Queen Margaret's brother, King Henry, to whom while she was at his court in England she had constantly misnamed the regent, now sent an envoy to harangue her on the evils of divorce. His hypocrisy is almost unbelievable seen in the light of what was to come.

But Henry, as ever, had a motive, in this case his wish to keep Angus in Scotland as the leader of the so-called 'English Party', which he had by then become. Henry's wife, Catherine of Aragon, more sympathetic to her sister-in-law, sent priest Father Bonaventura to advise Queen Margaret to endure her misfortunes as best she could.

Lord Dacre, however, knew her only too well; in writing to Cardinal Wolsey, he called Margaret's conduct scandalous. In a further letter to Queen Margaret herself, he accused her of over familiararity with Sir James Hamilton, an illegitimate son of Arran and a notorious womaniser with whom she had ridden alone, at dead of night, from Edinburgh to her palace of Linlithgow.

Albany arrived bringing not only a force of soldiers but also a large sum of money from France, sent by King Francis I, to induce the Scottish Council to support the Aulde Alliance. Angus, who had been in Edinburgh, opposed his wife's determination to divorce him and took refuge in Tantallon or, it is said, in a church somewhere on the Borders.

From whichever place he was in hiding, he sent his uncle Gavin Douglas, the Bishop of Dunkeld, to King Henry to suggest his willingness to head an alliance against Queen Margaret and the regent if support from England could be gained. Gavin Douglas, ageing and in poor health, took ten days to reach the English Court. Henry, however, wasted no time in writing to the Scottish Council to denounce the divorce of his sister and, with the threat of renewed war, demand the dismissal of Albany.

Gavin Douglas died shortly afterwards, his illness aggravated by the stress of travelling in mid-winter. Angus, bereft of his support, supposedly tried to become reconciled to his wife; on the pretext that she was showing him forgiveness, she prevailed upon Albany to send him to France as an ambassador, on the promise that his now known treachery would be forgiven.

The story that Angus and his brother George, unconscious after consuming drugged wine, were put aboard a ship for France bears no credence. However, both are known to have been in or around the French Court for a period of about three years. Angus apparently took his daughter Margaret with him. Nothing is heard of her in Scotland during that time. That she went to France seems likely in view of the fact that she was later known to speak fluent French. She was certainly not with her mother, as is proved by a letter the queen wrote from Edinburgh on 25 November 1524 in which, amongst many complaints against her husband, she adds that 'he would not suffer our own daughter to remain with us for our comfort'.[2]

It was shortly after this that the Regent Albany, having quarrelled with Queen Margaret again, finally returned to France. On news of his departure, Angus came back to Scotland with his daughter. This is proved by a letter from Catherine of Aragon to her mother begging that she would not disparage 'the fair daughter she had by my Lord Anguish [sic]', whose legitimacy was under question.[3] Queen Margaret responded, not to Catherine but to Margaret's godfather Wolsey, writing that because she had made a legal marriage to Angus, their daughter could not be called illegitimate. The edict was endorsed by Archbishop Beaton in a clause of Queen Margaret's divorce, finally granted in 1528.

By its terms Angus retained the custody of his daughter, by then 13 years old. Despite having contributed nothing towards the costs of her upbringing, her mother nonetheless promised her as a bride to the Earl of Moray as a means of achieving his allegiance.

On his return from France in 1524, Angus is known to have stayed first at his castle of Boncle, from where he could escape to England across the border. From there he wrote to Queen Margaret, still technically his wife, to try to make reconciliation. This was a mere formality: word had reached him that, despite her looks being ruined by smallpox, Queen Margaret had found a new lover in the form of Harry Stewart, a brother of Lord Avondale and one of her own guard. On his letter being returned unopened, as he had expected, he took the action he had already planned.

Margaret now lived largely at Tantallon Castle. Her father, chief of the Red Douglasses, saw to it that she was treated as a princess, which, as the daughter of the Queen of Scotland, she was entitled to be. Her biographer Agnes Strickland, on the evidence of a letter from Lord Eure to Cardinal Wolsey, states that it was at this time that Margaret, aware of her own importance, developed the 'imperious manner' she afterwards maintained throughout her life.

Certainly, from all that is known of her, it appears that Margaret inherited her father's stature rather than her mother's, who was small and, in later years, stout. Slim and with striking colouring, she was taller than most women of her time.

Haughty she may have been but Margaret was certainly a young Amazon, riding a horse with perfect balance, with a falcon carried on her wrist. The bird was one of her famous Tantallon hawks, bred specifically for hunting and famed as far as England for their power and beauty in flight. Margaret rode with her father, an expert horsemen and falconer himself. Together they raced over the gently rising ground above Tantallon, Margaret loving the thrill of it, her red hair streaming in the wind. Before them, hounds, noses to the turf, flushed birds from reeds and long grass. At sight of one rising for the sky, she would free her hawk from its jesses to let it fly in pursuit. She was, so her father claimed, as good a rider and falconer, if not better, than most of his men.

4

THE BATTLE
FOR THE KING

Yet Angus was seldom at Tantallon. King Henry had brought him back from France expressly to head the English Party in Scotland against the French.

On 1 August 1524, King James, now 12 years old, was present at the council that brought Albany's governorship officially to an end. On 5 August James signed a letter to his 'derrest and richt inteirlye weilbe-lufit uncle, the king of Inglande', telling him that he had ended the control of Albany 'under quhais governans oure realme and lieges hes bene richt evill demanyt'.[1] Following this, in September, arrangements were made for a Scottish embassy to go to England to conclude a treaty of peace. King Henry actually paid for 200 soldiers as a bodyguard for the young king of Scotland, and having done so, he sent two English residents to Edinburgh.

Despite this ostentatious display of concern for the security of his nephew, Henry met strong opposition in Scotland. Forming up against him were James Beaton, Archbishop of St Andrews and five of his bishops. They, along with Archibald Campbell, 4th Earl of Argyll; Argyll's cousin George Gordon, de facto Earl of Moray; and John Stuart, 3rd Earl of Lennnox, the grandson of James II, remained loyal to the Aulde Alliance with France.

Along with the Bishop of Aberdeen, Beaton was actually imprisoned for his intransigence but his nephew David, arriving from France, brought new hope to the Francophiles with a message of support from King Francis.

King Henry had sent his envoy, Doctor Magnus, Archdeacon of the East Riding of Yorkshire, to his sister at Holyrood in an attempt to dissuade her from divorce. Writing from there to Cardinal Wolsey on 16 November 1524, Magnus told him how Angus, riding to Edinburgh with the Earl of Lennox, Scott of Buccleuch and 400 Border cavalry, had contrived to scale the walls of the city and open one of the gates. Together with Queen Margaret, at Holyrood he had heard the screams of people fleeing before the swords of horsemen galloping wildly through the streets. Next he had been told that Angus had reached the Mercat Cross, from where he had ordered his herald to proclaim that he had come to take control of the government and to keep the peace.

Doctor Magnus, trying to mediate with Queen Margaret over the subject of her divorce, was told by her to mind his own business and be gone. Facing an emergency at Holyrood, the queen, abetted by her son the king, showed all the courage she possessed in defying her alienated husband. Knowing that she could not reach Edinburgh Castle because he held the Royal Mile, she ordered the two small cannons at Holyrood to be fired. A priest, an old woman and two merchant sailors were unlucky enough to be killed.

Later in the day Angus and Lennox, on the orders of the young king, left the city of Edinburgh for the Douglas castle of Dalkeith. Magnus was then able to describe to Wolsey how, by torchlight, King James, his mother (with a servant carrying her jewels) and the men and women of both their households rode up the hill to Edinburgh castle under the escort of Harry Stewart (rumoured to be the queen's paramour), in command of their royal guards.

A bizarre situation then developed in which the king, Queen Margaret and the Earl of Arran held the castle of Edinburgh, and Angus and Lennox the town. In February the estates named Angus as one of the queen's counsellors, and subsequently, with the earls of Lennox and Argyll, he controlled the ruling of the government.

This was enough to throw his estranged wife Queen Margaret into collusion with the French party, now headed by Arran, who felt himself ostracised by the English.

On 3 August the council issued a declaration that the queen would lose all authority unless she agreed to abide by the ruling of the lords of whom it was comprised. By now it had been arranged that the king should remain in the care of each of the leading lords in turn. Angus would take the first period, lasting until November, at which point, by firmly refusing to release him, he held him hostage for his power. In June of the following year of 1525 he issued a statement to the effect that all government was now in the king's hands, in fact meaning his own.

Angus then made a demonstration of necromancy oblivious to the fury of his foes. In July he removed the great seal from Archbishop Beaton, before taking the office of chancellor for himself. His uncle Archibald Douglass became treasurer and provost of Edinburgh; his brother George – ever a menacing presence by his side – was created master of the household; James Douglas of Drumlanrig was made master of the wine cellar; and James Douglas of Parkhead was created master of the larder.

Now regarded as a dictator, Angus was increasingly resented by Argyll and Lennox, with whom initially he had formed a triumvirate of power.

Backed by the queen, Moray and Glencairn, together with others, tried to organise the king's rescue. The first attempt, near Melrose, was made by Scott of Buccleuch. It failed, but on 4 September 1527 John, Earl of Lennox led an army to Linlithgow. Defeated by Arran at a battle which took place at Linlithgow Bridge, Lennox, despite having actually surrendered, was treacherously stabbed to death by Sir James Hamilton, the man with whom the queen had ridden from Linlithgow to Edinburgh alone and so secretly at night.

Rivalry between the families of Lennox and Hamilton had existed for over sixty years. Princess Mary, daughter of James II, had married James, first Lord Hamilton, as already described, by whom she had a son and a daughter. The son was created Earl of Arran, while the daughter married the second Earl of Lennox. Thus, through the laws of primogeniture, Arran had the better claim to the monarchy should the existing line fail. But his heir was doubtfully legitimate. The Lennoxes' offspring was unquestionably lawful and therefore they claimed predominance in the line of inheritance to the throne. This rivalry, always hostile, was further inflamed by this murder into a deadly dispute, destined to cause destruction to both the families involved.

Angus was now so feared and hated that hardly a single earl attended the council. But he remained omnipotent as long as the king stayed a prisoner in his hands. His brother George, arrogant with pride, boasted quite openly that 'should the king's body be torn apart in a rescue attempt, the Douglasses would still keep one part of it.'[2]

James thus remained in captivity until, in May 1528, he managed to liaise secretly with his mother, who alerted the governor of Stirling Castle to be prepared for his approach. At Falkland Palace, under cover of the night, he crept down the stairs and out to the stables. Disguised as a groom, he rode at full speed to Stirling, where the guards on watch at the castle raised the portcullis as had been previously arranged. Galloping beneath it into the castle courtyard, the young King of Scotland was free.

On 6 July King James entered Edinburgh at the head of a large concourse of nobles. Expecting at least some resistance, they found only acclamation from the people in the streets who watched them pass. Warned of their coming four days previously, Angus had already disappeared. On 13 July he was summoned for treason; in September, to the blast of a trumpet, as a herald proclaimed banishment, he was put to the horn.

5

Hunted as an Outlaw

His lands and his titles proscribed, Angus holed himself up in Tantallon, prepared to withstand a siege. With him, in addition to his bodyguard and the garrison, were his daughter, Margaret, and the Douglas relations who looked after her. The older women were apprehensive, voicing their fear in whispers to each other so that the child should not be alarmed. Their caution was quite unnecessary. To Margaret herself it was an adventure, one she would share with her father, who, whatever their enemies attempted, she knew would always keep her safe.

Excited by all the commotion, she watched as the well-practised ritual for preparation against a blockade began. Provisions were dragged into the courtyard on horse-drawn carts to be stored in the vaulted cellars, cold enough to preserve them for months. They included not only sacks of flour and tubs of salted meat but fish and young gannets, brought by boat across the short strip of sea from the Bass.

Tantallon was better equipped that most castles to withstand prolonged assault. Thanks to the foresight of Earl William, who 200 years earlier had raised water to the courtyard well, they were safe from dying of thirst. Also it had better defences than many other buildings where walls lacked the sealing strength of lime. In the towers of the curtain wall, marksmen waited, their muskets primed; they listened attentively for a shout from the sentries on guard on the ramparts of the castle, from where, unless in mist or darkness, they could see many miles inland and across the North Sea, as far as the Isle of May and beyond the Firth of Forth.

The massive walls of Tantallon, in places 15ft deep, gave a sense of security to those within their protection. The castle had withstood attack for so long that it seemed invulnerable to assault. But cannons, brought to Scotland from Guelders some sixty years earlier as part of the dowry of the Flemish bride of James II, had destroyed the immense Douglas stronghold of Threep on an island in the Border River Dee. And now that king's great grandson, also James, was rumoured to be gathering an army.

Inevitably, cannons would come from Edinburgh Castle, dragged by teams of oxen across the nearly flat land below the Firth of Forth. The certainty of this happening gripped the minds of the people in Tantallon with an ever-increasing fear.

The sentries on the ramparts, straining their eyes into the distance behind the Berwick Law, were the first to hear it: a murmur in the far distance, born on the east wind. Looking at each other in puzzlement, they tried to make out what it was, this strange rhythmic noise such as they had never heard …

'Ding doon Tantallon.' The drums of the king's army were beating the first known regimental march. King James is said to have sent an army of 8,000 men to overcome the strongest defence on Scotland's east coast. The earthworks, dug by his soldiers, can still be traced to this day.

Angus himself rode off to the Borders before the castle came within range of the approaching guns. With his intimate knowledge of the country, he knew the best ways to escape. Before leaving he told his daughter Margaret exactly what she must do.

Following her father's instructions, Margaret waited until the sun sank behind North Berwick Law. Then, in the deepening darkness, Margaret, her aunts and a few of their servants, clutching their most precious possessions, scrambled down the rough stone stairs. The steps, dangerous and slippery, were just visible in the light of burning torches as they climbed to the sea-gate, on the same level as the dungeons entombed in the castle's foundations in the cliff. Opening the gate, a cold wind hit them, laced with the smell of the sea. The tide was high and the drop to the boat awaiting them, with men ready at the oars, was only a few feet. Margaret found it easy, agile at thirteen years, but her aunts, armed down by men of the garrison, tried to subdue their cries of fear.

The exact place of their landing can only be guessed at today. Possibly it was below Whitekirk, where the Pope's nuncio, sent on a mission to James I, had come ashore a hundred years before. All that is known for certain is that they wandered like gypsies, sleeping in barns or whatever shelter could be found. For Margaret it may have been an adventure; for her aunts it must have been terrifying and exhausting in the extreme. Not for a moment could they relax, feeling themselves safe in any way. They were always watching, listening for the bands of soldiers which Margaret's half-brother, the king, had sent to look for her (which is what they had learned from the few local people to whom they dared to speak).

For six months from September 1528, the families of the Borders were involved in civil war. Even as Margaret's brother, King James, was holding an assizes on the Borders, Angus took the town of Coldringham from the Homes. But, as he must have been aware, he had powerful enemies biding their time to take a vicious revenge.

Afraid for his daughter's safety, on 5 September Angus sent a messenger across the River Tweed to ask Roger Lascelles, steward of the Earl of Northumberland and Governor of Norham Castle, on behalf of himself and Archibald Douglas to give sanctuary both to his own daughter, Margaret, and to the latter's wife.

The request is verified in a letter from Roger Lascelles to Henry VIII dated 8 September 1528, in which he tells him that 'The Earl of Angus hath expulsed the Lord Home and his brother out of Coldinghame, and there doth remain himself.' Significantly, he continues 'and now the Earl hath sent unto your Grace's castle of Norham, the Lady Margaret his daughter (which he had by the Queen your sister) who here doth remain until such time as I shall know further of your Grace's pleasure'.[1] Lascelles protested strongly, writing that the castle was in no way fit to lodge anyone, let alone high-born ladies. Water dripped through the whole building, from the roof down to the dungeons.

Norham Castle, on the English side of the Tweed, taken from the English by James IV, had returned to them after the battle of Flodden in which the king had died. It was one of the safest places of refuge as long as the truce with England should last. Standing high above the river and with a steep slope to the north, a deep ravine to the west and an artificial moat crossed by a drawbridge to the east and south, the castle was further protected by a portcullis above the entrance to the outer ward of the keep.

While still in Tantallon, an old servant of the Douglas family, Alexander Pringle, had revealed to Margaret that her mother, to whom she was now no more than a bargaining factor, was planning to marry her off to a brother of Harry Stewart, by now her third husband, following her recent divorce. John Stewart, captain by royal appointment of Doune Castle in Perthshire, was the man chosen by Queen Margaret to wed the daughter who, for the last seven years, she had not even seen.

Told of the state of Norham Castle, her mother saw a chance to get her daughter back, protesting that she was living under rough conditions that were not only unsuitable to her position but probably a risk to her health. Writing yet again to Doctor Magnus on 1 November 1528, she blamed Angus for innumerable wrongs.

> We, for tender love and welfare of the Earl of Anguish [*sic*] and of his house, moved of good mind, humanit us to solemnize matrimony with him, trusting that he of his nobility should not have forgot that we for him was exiled from the government of this realm, the most of our goods perforce withholden, our houses and possessions always retrained from our use, and we desolate of remedy. We, not regarding these inconveniences, always procured the Earl's weal and safety, first in this realm, and hereafter in our dearest brother's realm in England. When it pleased our dearest brother, Henry VIII, to convey us at great expense into the realm of Scotland again, within short space after the said Earl behaved himself quite uncourteously to us, and also suffered his friends to do in like manner; and entirely, since that time, he and they have done perverse to our displeasure. In special, these three years past, having no consideration to our person, honour, nor weal, but always putting all in gueppart [jeopardy] which were piteous and great marvel to report, and aitouce [twice] would not suffer our ane daughter to remain with us to our comfort, who would not have been dishrest [distressed], she being with us.[2]

Norham Castle, although so well defended, was not a safe haven for long. During the hard won peace, Henry's warden, Lord Dacre, did not want to upset the good relationship by helping fugitives from Scotland who were technically rebels to the king's dearest nephew, the King of Scotland. Told by the governor that they must leave, Margaret and the women with her, who included it seems a governess called Isobal Hopper, became vagrants once more. Moving from one house or castle to another, wherever they could find a roof above their heads, and perhaps sometimes where they could not, they were homeless while fighting continued on the Borders between the families involved in feuds.

Nothing more is known of Margaret until a year later, when her father took her to Sir Thomas Strangeways, the Captain of Berwick. By this time her clothes were nothing but rags. Those of the Douglas ladies who were with her were likewise so threadbare that Captain Strangeways took them in out of pity, on the promise made by her father that he would pay for their keep. Another main reason for doing so was that Margaret herself told him that she was Cardinal Wolsey's godchild, and as a young man Strangeways had been employed in Wolsey's household.

Sir Thomas, much perplexed by the sudden influx of women, sent the Carlisle herald to Wolsey to tell him what had occurred. Wolsey, who himself was facing a crisis in his refusal to condole the king's divorce from Queen Catherine, replied by the herald telling him to retain his guest as was consistent with her comfort. Three months passed, and with no word of Margaret and her household of several women and a man being moved, Strangeways wrote again to the Cardinal.

Dating his letter 'From Berwick, the 26th July 1529', he asked if he could give her more liberty, having been warned by her father that unless he took good care of her 'she might be stolen and withdrawn into Scotland'. Nonetheless, despite these restrictions, 'she was never merrier and more pleased and content than she is now, as she ofttimes repeats'. Howsoever, along with her servants and several visitors, not to mention her father, she had now been with him for all of three months and he had not, as had been promised, been paid.[3]

Margaret's awkward situation, though she seems to have been happy in the care of the custodian of Berwick, remained for a time unsolved. Eventually, however, her aunt, the beautiful Mary, Duchess of Suffolk and former queen of France, was told, presumably by Wolsey, of the straights to which the girl was reduced. Subsequently, Mary prevailed on her brother King Henry to allow her to come to England, on the promise that she would look after their homeless and neglected niece.

Forthwith Margaret travelled to England, escorted by Captain Thomas Strangeways himself. She is known to have stayed with her aunt over Christmas, and one wonders what the gentle, sophisticated Mary made of this long-legged girl with a tangle of red gold hair and who, now on the verge of womanhood, walked and rode like a man. Still more must she have puzzled over her niece's south Scots accent, which, so unlike the musical tongue of the French, was quite uncouth to the ear. The duchess did her best to tame her, and Margaret, unused as she was to the tender care of a woman so different from her ever grumbling aunts, began to enjoy the warmth and luxury of her new, if temporary, home.

It must have been with genuine sadness that she was forced to leave, when, at the beginning of the following year, 1529, Henry ordered that she should be taken to Beaulieu in Essex to live with his daughter Princess Mary.

6

THE COUSINS

To the girl of 15, used as she was to rough living in draughty, insanitary Border castles, it must have seemed that she was entering fairyland as her coach rumbled up the mile-long tree-lined drive.

Her uncle, the king, had bought the estate some fourteen years before in 1517 from Sir Thomas Boleyn, father of Anne, upon whom Henry had already set his eye. Determined that his heiress, Princess Mary, although at that time just a year old, should have all the splendour of her status as his heir, the king had transformed the building into a palace.

Beaulieu, as Henry called it, meaning beautiful place, was certainly imposing to behold. Built round no less than eight courtyards, it was fronted with a façade that was 550ft in length, in the centre of which stood two massive gatehouse towers. Henry had used the latest style of architecture, imported from Rome, based on a series of perfect squares. This was the first of his palaces, created to emphasise his might. Traces of its magnificence were discovered when in 2009, nearly 500 years later, Channel 4's *Time Team* came to investigate the site whilst making a documentary. Discovering an intricate system of Tudor drains where the western range would have stood, they conjectured that this must have been the nursery built for the little princess.

Now Princess Mary was no longer in the nursery but had moved into the great state rooms of the palace. Impressed as she had been by the comfort and splendour of her aunt's house, Margaret had never before known or seen such magnificence as the interior of the building to which, as a guest, she now came.

Instead of the bare draughty walls of the Border keeps she was used to, with pieces of hide stuck into holes and cracks to keep out draughts, she now lived in rooms hung with tapestries, glowing with a myriad of colours, and heated with fires. Now, instead of eating mainly with her fingers, she dined using cutlery off silver and gold plates. Most luxurious of all were the hip-baths. Used as she was to washing in cold water drawn from burns and rivers, which were sometimes even covered with ice, the warm water, scented with rose oil, was something of which she had dreamed. In her new robes, paid for by her uncle Henry, she learned to walk with short steps, to curtsey and even, under a dancing master, to do stately pavanes and gavottes.

By the time of her arrival, her cousin, the Princess Mary, just a few months younger than herself, had reached the age of 14. The contrast between the two girls could not have been greater, both in physical appearance and in character. Mary was small and dark haired. She had the sallow skin of her Spanish descent and was so thin that her collarbones showed clearly above the square-cut bodices of the dresses fashionable at that time. Most notice-ably, she spoke with a voice so deep that those hearing but not seeing her might take her for a man.

Mary did not have good health. Her frequent headaches were brought on to some extent by too much reading, peering short-sightedly into books. Also, aware of her physical weaknesses, her lack of self-confidence made her so shy that she feared showing affection even to those she most loved.

Margaret, on the other hand, was tall, with the red gold hair of her Tudor mother and skin still tanned from riding for long hours exposed to wind, rain and sun. She was also bold and, some claimed, imperious in her manner. Moreover, she was openly outspoken and unafraid to speak her mind. Defiant of criticism, she nonetheless showed great deference to Lady Salisbury, who, besides being Mary's godmother, was both a near relation and a devoted Catholic, these being the reasons why King Henry had appointed her as head of his daughter's household. Now a dowager of 63, this formidable, if saintly, lady was, as the daughter of the 1st Duke of Clarence, the last of the royal house of Plantagenet which had ended with the death of Richard III.

A peeress in her own right, she had been married to Sir William Pole, a cousin of Henry VII, but had been left so penniless on his death, with five children to support, that the king had paid for her husband's funeral. Later, however, when an act of parliament had restored her family's lands, she had become one of the richest women in England. A lady-in-waiting to Catherine of Aragon, her high birth and irreproachable character had proved her to be eminently suitable to take charge of the princess, who, until a son should be born to him, remained Henry's heir. Nonetheless, her own son, Reginald Pole, paid for by Henry to study theology in France and Italy during his family's penury, had subsequently incurred his wrath. Offered the Archbishopric of York if he would support his divorce from Catherine, Reginald had stubbornly refused, returning to self exile abroad.

He had left his mother under suspicion. Many Catholic families in the north of England were known to be hostile to the divorce. Margaret Salisbury, a direct descendant of the Plantagenets, was in Henry's eyes a likely figurehead in the very possible outcome of a civil war.

Pious as Lady Salisbury, Princess Mary's governess, Margaret Bryant, had been with her almost since she was born. Mary, a natural linguist, was now fluent in French and Latin and of course in Spanish, her mother's native tongue. Margaret must have learnt at least some French if, as is thought, she had stayed in France with her father for a period of about three years. Nonetheless, her education otherwise had been of the most basic kind. She spoke with the strong accent of the Lowland Scots, and both her cousin Mary and her governess, now teaching Margaret as well, found it almost as bad as deciphering a foreign language in their efforts to understand what she said.

The ladies of Mary's household, used as they were to refinement, must have listened in horror and amazement to Margaret's stories of her adventures with her father in the Scottish Borders. Hearing of her wanderings from one rough fort to another and of how at times both she and her aunts had slept in barns and even open fields, they must have shivered at the thought.

For Margaret, who could barely speak the King's English, the struggle to learn both Latin and French, the languages then highly essential to anyone in royal circles, must have been great. Hardly less onerous were the sewing lessons, beginning with seams and then progressing to tiny stitches of embroidery. Margaret, glancing from the windows, and probably pricking her thumb, must have longed to be out on the back of a horse instead of being forced to sit stitching in a room, over heated, even in summer, by a fire.

Yet frustrated as she then was by a lack of freedom, she was to look back on those days at Beaulieu as some of the happiest of her life. One thing above all that made it so was the joy shown by Mary on her arrival. Used as she was to loneliness in the austere atmosphere of an ageing household, dominated by its strict chatelaine, Mary rejoiced in the company of this strong, confident cousin who had lived a life so adventurous compared to her own. Together they talked of their ambitions, of their hopes of soon finding suitors and inevitably, as most girls do, of the so far hidden joys of sex and of whom, in their own young opinions, were the most desirable and dashing men at court.

In Mary's eyes no one equalled her father, whom she openly adored. But sometimes her moods were saddened, and as they walked together in the garden, their duennas trailing behind, Mary whispered to Margaret that she was deeply afraid. Her father had a new mistress. There had, of course, been others, notably Bessie Blount, who had actually borne him a son. But this woman was different. She was scheming and determined to get him so that she could be queen. Margaret tried to console her, but Mary was a realist and she cried at night for her mother, whom she so steadfastly loved.

Mary wept in bewilderment, confused in her loyalty to her parents, both of whom she adored. To Margaret she told her amazement that anyone as brave and good as her father, whom she idolised, could be so cruel to her mother because she had failed to give him a living son. Her mother had tried so hard to achieve what was her wish as well as his own. She had so nearly done so when her first son, another Henry, had lived for fifty-two days. Devastated by his death, as were both his parents, Henry had then made her regent when he went to France with his army. The Scots, seizing at the chance of his absence, had been about to invade, whereupon, despite being heavily pregnant, she had ridden north in full armour, on an eye-catching white horse. After the battle of Flodden she had actually sent Henry a bloodstained coat, reputed to be that of James IV.

She had been so brave, Mary said, and was it surprising that under these circumstances she had given birth prematurely to another son who lived but a few hours? Yet another had been stillborn and two other girls had died within days. Thus it was only Mary who had survived as her father's heir.

The injustice done to her mother, so much loved by the people of England, was almost more than she could endure.

It was Margaret who should have been Henry's daughter, as Mary very well knew. Margaret was so strong and courageous that she could hold even the strongest pulling horse, while she herself was so nervous that she could only manage an ambling palfrey or, better still, a docile mule. Margaret, with her red gold hair and the height which gave her such presence, was every inch a Tudor, while Mary, with her Spanish descent, had very little resemblance to the statuesque father whose approval she so desperately craved.

The first notice of King Henry's attention to his niece 'Marget', as was his pet name for her, appears in the Privy Purse Expenses, where it is noted that the king ordered £6 13s 4d to be given to 'the Lady Margaret Anguish to disport herself this Christmas'. The gift, although probably to buy material for seamstresses to make her new clothes, would also have been designed to allow her to give the customary presents to her servants. In addition it was essential to have enough money to gamble at cards, then such a major distraction in most large houses in the land.

Margaret spent that Christmas of 1530 with her uncle King Henry at Greenwich Palace. It proved to be a family gathering for with them was Mary's mother, Catherine of Aragon, for the last time presiding as queen.

The king is reported to have shown great affection for his niece, admiring both her striking looks and her bold spirit, with which, when they went hawking, she rode even faster than did he. Also, trained by her father with the Tantallon hawks, she could fly the falcons and make them return to her, to the admiration of even the experts who thought falconry the right of men.

Aware of his fondness towards her, she begged him to grant her the great favour of allowing her father and her other uncle, his brother George Douglas, almost his amanuensis, to come to court. Henry acquiesced, as ever with his own ends in view. The Privy Purse proves that on 15 December in the following year of 1531, the Earl of Angus, on leaving Greenwich Palace, was given the sum of £46 13s 4d; at the same time, his daughter, as in the previous year, received money 'for playing at cards and other diversions of the season'.

In addition to this, when the court moved to Waltham, Margaret's uncle, George Douglas, to ensure his loyalty, received £100. Henry, who never did anything for nothing, had now seen a way to achieve his declared intention of becoming the ruler of Scotland: subsidising the Douglasses to confront the Regent Albany, then the Scottish agent in France, with no less than £1,000.

Specifically, it was stated that the king's benefice was 'to supply the sustenance of both the Earl of Angus and his daughter'. This meant that for the first time in her life Margaret was freed from the charity of relations. Now, within the precincts of Beaulieu, she could have her own household, independent of anyone else.

Firstly, and most importantly, she had her chaplain, a Roman Catholic priest named Charles. In addition, in charge of her wardrobe was Peter, who was 'wonderfully skilled with a needle', and below him another man named Hervey, as well as three maids. Outside in the huge block of stables, to look after her horses, she had three grooms.

No one expressed more joy over the change in Margaret's fortunes than did Princess Mary, who, in addition to being her first cousin and almost the same age, had become her closest friend and confidante. Mary was relieved to know that Margaret had at least some substance at a time when her own family conflicts threatened the stability of her life.

7

'THE KING'S WICKED INTENTION'

The Christmas spent at Greenwich Palace in the previous year of 1531 was proving to be the last period of happiness that Mary was to know for some time. It was now six years since her father, King Henry, had set his heart on marrying the auburn-haired, black-eyed Anne Boleyn, then a lady-in-waiting to her mother, the queen.

Determined to acquire an annulment of his marriage on the grounds that she had formerly been married to his elder brother, Arthur – which he conveniently interpreted to be wrong in the eyes of God – he had tried, unsuccessfully, to make her retire to a nunnery. Upon her refusing to do so, he had then sent his secretary, William Knight, to Pope Clement VII to sue for an annulment on the grounds that the dispensation, issued by the previous Pope, had been granted on false pretences.

Much to the sorrow of both Princess Mary and Margaret Douglas, his goddaughter, both grateful for of his kindness, Cardinal Wolsey, castigated for his failure to gain the king's ambition, had been dismissed as chancellor in 1529. Incensed, he had then begun plotting against Anne Boleyn, communicating with the Pope to that end. When discovered, Henry had ordered his arrest on a charge of treachery, but he had died of terminal cancer before being forced to stand trial.

Soon came rumours of the king's determination on divorce. Mary, tight lipped in her sorrow, began to refuse to eat. Margaret, disturbed by Mary's misery and concerned for the Spanish queen, whom even through short acquaintance she had learned to love so well, tried only to help her cousin by assuring her that divorce would be prohibited by the Pope in Rome. Lady Salisbury, devoted both to the queen and to the Catholic faith they shared, went about straight faced, while the household over which she presided waited in fear for news.

Soon after that Christmas at Greenwich, Queen Catherine was ordered to leave the court. Shortly, her old rooms in Greenwich Palace were given to Anne Boleyn. In the New Year Mary went to visit her mother, who was now living in The More at Rickmansworth in Hertfordshire. This magnificent mansion, on the south side of the flood plain of the Colne Valley, dated originally from the thirteenth century and had been rebuilt by Cardinal Wolsey. He had added two wings and the formal gardens in 1522. Nonetheless, despite her new home being one of the grandest houses in England, large enough to hold her 200 servants, Catherine was deeply resentful at being moved from her old apartments in Greenwich Palace to make way for Anne Boleyn. Voicing her indignation in a letter to the Holy Roman Emperor, Charles V, she told him that: 'My tribulations are so great, my life so disturbed by the plans daily invented to further the King's wicked intention … my treatment is what God knows, that it is enough to shorten ten lives, much more mine.'[1]

Henry was determined to keep his still not divorced wife and their daughter apart, convinced, with some reason, that Catherine was plotting against him and that she meant to involve Mary in her schemes. To make matters worse, he then discovered that Catherine was carrying on a secret correspondence with the Pope, who ordered him to put Anne away and take Catherine back. Apoplectic with rage, Henry declared that neither the Pope nor the Holy Roman Emperor had any right to dictate to the king, now God's anointed head of the Church of England. Catherine, accused of conspiracy, was moved from the More to Hatfield, built by Cardinal Morton but seized by Henry from the Church.

Soon afterwards, when the Archbishop of Canterbury, William Warham, died, the Boleyn's own chaplain, Thomas Cranmer, was appointed to fill his place. On 23 May 1533, Cranmer, convening over a special court to debate the validity of King Henry's marriage to Queen Catherine, declared it to be illegal on the grounds of her previous marriage to his brother. Forthwith he proclaimed the legality of his marriage to Anne Boleyn.

Princess Mary and all of her household reacted with horror to the news. Deeply saddened by the callous insult to her mother, she refused, as did Lady Salisbury, to acknowledge the new queen. Further distress was to follow when, less than a month later, it was learned that Mary, Duchess of Suffolk – the Queen Duchess, as she was always known – had died at her home, Westhorpe Hall in Suffolk, on 25 June.

Both Princess Mary and Lady Margaret Douglas, her nieces who had loved her, were deeply saddened by her death; Margaret in particular remembering how when, homeless and an outcast from Scotland, she had welcomed her to Westhorpe in that winter of 1526.

Margaret was still at Beaulieu at the time of the Duchess' death, and summer was turning to autumn when they heard that on 7 September a daughter, not the longed for son, had been born to the king and queen.

On 1 October King Henry made the new princess his heir. Declaring his elder daughter Mary illegitimate on the excuse that his marriage to her mother had been illegal, he forbade her to call herself princess. Mary, not surprisingly, reacted with such violent fury that her father, whose temper she had inherited, sent her to live at Hertford while forbidding her to see her mother, lest the two should conspire against him.

The fact that Mary was now proclaimed illegitimate meant that Margaret Douglas, second only to the newly born Princess Elizabeth, was Henry's nearest heir. His new queen, conscious of her position, required the attendance of the daughter of the king's eldest sister, the Queen of Scotland, as her right. Subsequently, without delay, Margaret was summoned to court.

Then at Beaulieu there was much commotion, with Margaret's servants running up and down the stairs, and to and fro the rooms. At last all her gowns and jewels were packed and carried downstairs to the carts and carriages in which she and her entourage would travel to London. Inevitably, she must have marvelled at the quantity and richness of possessions acquired since her arrival three years before, penniless and with hardly a decent gown to her name.

Amongst those who watched the departure of the girl whose deportment and manners had shocked everyone when she first came, was the governess she had shared with Princess Mary, as she had then been known. Dignified as ever, in black robes and an old-fashioned headdress shaped like a tent above her face, Lady Salisbury may have been sad to see Margaret – who had arrived like a tousled haired gypsy and who now was second in line to the throne – leave the protection of her care. Margaret Salisbury's own father and brother had been executed by Henry VII for the danger of their nearness to the throne; she must have murmured a prayer for this vibrant young woman, who, despite all her warnings, still had no real knowledge of the peril that awaited her in, what to Lady Salisbury, was the cesspit of the new queen's court.

8

So Much Destroyed
By Death

Margaret was certainly surprised by the personality of Queen Anne. Instead of the frivolous young woman who, through gossip and Lady Salisbury's dire predictions, she had come to expect, she found someone who was serious and intelligent, with a very good knowledge of the political situation both at home and abroad. Anne was not only astute, she was also a fashion icon of her day. During her early years spent in France, she had learned how to dress with great style. It was she who had introduced the latest French fashions, including the entrancingly pretty headdresses of snoods bordered with pearls; one she had worn to hold back the long auburn hair, famously reaching to her waist, so long that she actually sat on it as she drove to York Place, where her wedding to the king had taken place on 25 January.

It was fortunate for Margaret that she now had some money to buy herself new gowns of satin and velvet, with the square necks cut low enough to give a provocative hint of a woman's breasts, as were presently in vogue.

If almost stupefied at first by the magnificence of the clothes of the men and women with whom she mingled in the rooms and corridors of Greenwich Palace, Margaret was quick to recognise a subtle atmosphere of mistrust.

Through the smiles, extravagant compliments and courtly gestures, her sharp mind perceived the undercurrents of jealousy and distrust. Men who bowed to each other or over a lady's hand would slide away unobtrusively to find quiet corners in which to confer so quietly that their whispers were drowned by the rustle of taffeta and silks.

Strange as she must at first have found it, Margaret did become accustomed to the routine of the court. The queen, surprisingly, belied her former reputation put about by her enemies of using her powers of duplicity and manipulation to ensnare the king. Queen Anne, to outward eyes, was now a model of virtue and restraint. She insisted on good behaviour, telling her ladies 'to take especiall regarde, and to omit nothing that may seem to apperteigne to honour'.[1] A fervent evangelist, she insisted that all of her household should attend a religious service every day. To encourage them in the Protestant faith, she gave each of them a book of Psalms in English. Soon she was reproaching her cousin Mary Shelton for using hers as a jotter for romantic verse. Mary was only one of the many young ladies inspired by the poet Thomas Wyatt, whose own work, amongst those of his protégées, is now in the Devonshire Manuscript of the British Museum. Amongst them are verses which for their levity were first ascribed to Anne Boleyn; now, analysis of the handwriting has proved them to be by Mary Shelton and Mary Howard, both cousins of Queen Anne and also, most significantly, by Margaret Douglas.

Surprisingly, the queen, so renowned as a merciless schemer, was a devoted mother: the little princess Elizabeth was kept with her as much as possible and lay on a velvet cushion on the floor beside her throne. When told that the princess must have her own household, she begged to be allowed to keep her at court, but in this matter Henry was adamant. Protocol must be maintained. Nonetheless, he did allow that the baby princess should have a young woman in charge of her, not, as so often happened, a matriarch with rigid, old-fashioned ideas.

It was three months after her arrival at court, when the Christmas festivities were just about to begin, that Margaret Douglas was told that she was to be first lady in Princess Elizabeth's own household at Hatfield in Hertfordshire. Taken there, away from her mother, the little princess was carried through the streets of London to show her to the people. Behind came her own household, headed by Margaret, together with a mounted escort of much of the nobility of England.

Reaching Hatfield, Margaret was soon to be informed that Princess Mary, now on her father's orders known only as the Lady Mary, was to join her infant half-sister's domain. Since Mary had been declared illegitimate, Margaret was now her superior in rank, but so close was their friendship that this was one of her many humiliations that Mary never resented. Margaret, for her part, was bitterly angry at the way in which Mary was treated. Allowed to keep none but a few of her own servants, she realised the full extent of her vulnerability as even the devoted Lady Salisbury, offering to serve her at her own expense, was ruthlessly told to be gone. Given only a back room, poorly furnished, in Hatfield House, Mary, eldest daughter of the King of England, was hardly more than a servant.

The new Queen Anne, devoted as she was to her own child, was bitterly jealous of her stepdaughter. The situation might have been eased had Mary acknowledged her as queen. But Mary did not. Small and thin as she was, Mary had all the stubbornness of the great figure of her father. Urged on by his new wife, Henry, although secretly admiring her spirit, so much akin to his own, tried by these means of degradation to break the defiance of this elder daughter. But Mary insisted that her mother still was queen. Still more insulting, she doggedly refused to acknowledge that he, despite an act of parliament, was head of the Church of England.

Confused and bewildered as to how to tackle Mary's obduracy, Henry ordered Anne's uncle and aunt, Sir John and Lady Shelton (parents of the poetess Mary), who had been put in charge of her, to try and starve her into submission. Secretly, she sent messages to her mother, whom she was not permitted to see but who somehow contrived to send her a letter, smuggled in by one of the few of her own servants whom she was allowed to keep.

When Henry visited his other daughter, the little Princess Elizabeth, Mary was locked into her room, where the windows were sealed with nails. Forbidden even to walk in the garden, she was left imprisoned at Hatfield when Princess Elizabeth, with her household, was moved to the different palaces of Hunsdon, Chelsea, Kensington and Havering Bower, both for the purpose of house cleaning and for a change of air.

Margaret, in addition to her duties as head of the princess' household, was also in attendance on Queen Anne. With her slim form and striking colouring, she quickly excited attention amongst the courtiers, most of whom, married or not, were always ready for the chance of a romance.

While spurning the advances of most of them, philanderers, as she knew them to be, she was attracted by one young man with whom she shared a love of verse.

Thomas Howard was the eighth child of the Duke of Norfolk, whose sister, Elizabeth, was the mother of Anne Boleyn. Thus, although being the second son of his father's second marriage, and therefore close to her in age, he was actually the uncle of Queen Anne, who by now was renowned for promoting her own relations at court. Having made a good match for her cousin Mary Howard to Henry's illegitimate son, whom he had created Duke of Richmond, she now set about trying to arrange another between Margaret Douglas and her young uncle.

In the meantime King Henry, on the suggestion of the queen, sent Thomas' elder brother, Lord William Howard, previously Princess Mary's chamberlain, to Scotland to win the compliance of Queen Margaret to what was presumed to be her daughter's imminent marriage. Both Margaret and Thomas were in waiting at Westminster Palace in the early months of 1536, where, although living in separate apartments, they were now committed to each other by a solemn act of betrothal; this amounted virtually to a secret marriage, which may even have taken place. At this point, King Henry, much under the influence of Anne, with whom he was still deeply in love, was acquiescent to their wish to marry.

On 11 March 1536 the king got his way: the Bill for the Dissolution of the Monasteries was passed. The money raised from this act proved to be the first reason for contention between Anne and Thomas Cromwell, with whom she had formerly been on good terms. While Anne wanted to spend the money on providing education and relief for the poor, Cromwell had other ideas for its use. Resentful of Anne's influence, he began to formulate a scheme by which to undermine her power.

Through her close attendance upon Anne at court, Margaret was to witness how it was her independence and persistent involvement in politics, rather than any lack of sexual charm or, as has been so persistently claimed, her failure to produce a male heir, which was to prove her downfall. Anne was a passionate believer in the reformed religion and it was she who encouraged Henry to make an alliance with Guelders, Cleves and the Schmalkaldic League with the object of making the Holy Roman Emperor Charles V's hold over the Netherlands almost untenable. Under her influence, Henry secretly financed Lübeck, a free Imperial state, but his sway in the politics of Europe diminished when the Duke of Oldenburg seized the throne of Denmark, which subsequently became allied to the Schmalkaldic League.

This was enough to make Cromwell change his mind about forming a Protestant alliance. Anne never forgave him and from this time on they became implacable enemies. Cromwell realised that she would destroy him with her hold over the king. He set about to ruin her by any possible means.

Cleverly, he began to implant suspicion into the king's mind, insinuating that it was now being put about that he ruled only through his wife. Henry did not need much persuasion. Anne's decisive character, shrewd remarks and ready wit which had once so intrigued him were now becoming an irritant, as Cromwell had rightly perceived.

It was on 18 April 1535 that Eustace Chapuys, the Vatican's ambassador and spymaster, received a special invitation from Henry to meet the queen. Chapuys had never met Anne, whom he refused to acknowledge as the king's wife and Queen of England. As predicted, he refused the summons but Cromwell, by subterfuge, arranged that he would find himself face to face with her soon afterwards. Overcome with embarrassment, the ambassador had no alternative but to bow to her in front of the whole court. Later, Chapuys had an interview with Henry, purportedly to deliver a message from his master, the Holy Roman Emperor, Charles V that he was willing to liaise with him against the French; during the interview he was unwise enough to raise the subject of the treatment of Princess Mary. Henry was furious, saying the emperor should mind his own business, and reminding him that as head of the Church of England he was now no longer obedient to the Pope. Having railed against the unfortunate legate, he then turned on Cromwell saying he had acted without his authority in arranging the meeting with the Queen.

Cromwell had hoped to humble Anne, but by the public abeyance of the Pope's ambassador and Henry's castigation of himself, he knew she had won the first round.

Nonetheless, thanks to Cromwell's insinuations, Henry had an uneasy mind. Not only did he perceive his wife to be a rival to his own power but, ageing and unattractive as he now knew himself to be, he began to imagine that he was being cuckolded by some of the young men with whom, through their official appointments, she was inevitably in contact at court.

Having forsworn the idea of a Protestant alliance, Cromwell then allied himself to the Seymours, who as hereditary Catholics disliked Anne for her Protestant convictions. On 3 March Edward Seymour was appointed to the Privy Chamber and forthwith contrived to draw the king's attention to his sister Jane, one of the queen's ladies-in-waiting, whose docile character made her the antithesis of Anne.

The court was at Greenwich Palace for the May Day festival, when, as contestants were jousting, thundering down the lists, Queen Anne was seen to drop a handkerchief, supposedly a secret sign to a lover.

Margaret, however, did not witness this. It is known from a letter from her former governess, Margaret Bryant, to Thomas Cromwell, that she was with Princess Elizabeth at Hunsdon, near Ware in Hertfordshire, during the trial and divorce of the unfortunate queen, who was beheaded in the Tower of London on 19 May.

Eleven days later, on 30 May, the king married Jane Seymour in the Queen's Closet, a room so called for Anne, in Whitehall Palace. Henry showed off his bride at the celebrations before they made a triumphal process down the Thames from Greenwich to the city. Guns were fired and trumpeters sounded volleys as the royal barge passed by. The Tower itself, where Anne Boleyn had been buried in the chapel less than three weeks before, was now festooned with banners, bright against the sombre walls.

On 15 June at the feast of Corpus Christi, the king rode to Westminster Abbey at the head of a procession. Behind came the pale, unobtrusive Queen Jane, who, although richly dressed and much bejewelled, could not outshine her chief lady-in-waiting, Lady Margaret Douglas, whose height and striking red hair caught the eye of most of the beholders. It was Margaret, who, as the king's niece, now took precedence over the daughters of the wives he had beheaded and divorced. Margaret, through rite of birth, as the second lady in the land, carried the queen's train throughout the succeeding ceremony.

9

'THE FAITHFULLEST LOVER THAT EVER WAS BORN'

A lthough high in favour with her uncle, Margaret was only too well aware that, unpredictable as he was, her own future was jeopardised to a perilous degree. The death of Queen Anne had robbed her lover, the queen's young uncle Thomas Boleyn, of his main support. The Boleyns and their adherents were now in disgrace. Both the princesses, Mary and Elizabeth, had been declared illegitimate and thus, until his long-awaited son was born, the Lady Margaret Douglas and her half-brother the King of Scotland remained the king's nearest heirs.

Told that it was totally out of the question for them to marry, Thomas and Margaret waited in terror, wondering if theirs would be the next heads to fall. A month passed before the expected happened as they were arrested and taken to the Tower. The trumped-up charge against them, ridiculous as it now seems, was of 'compassing treason against the King, for taking each other as man and wife'. Immured in separate parts of the building, they waited to hear the sentence that one or both must die.

Margaret was lodged in the part wherein lived the lieutenant of the Tower. It is known that from the window of one of the rooms allotted to her, she could look down on the site of the scaffold where the grass was still stained with the blood of Anne Boleyn. Whether this was deliberate, directly ordered by the king to frighten her, will never be known. But if so, it would be in character with a man for whom terror was a way of extracting both secrets and obedience from his victims, as is elsewhere proved.

Margaret most certainly had the charge against Thomas read out to her by a herald, sent by the king to the Tower.

That the Lord Thomas Howard, brother to Thomas, now Duke of Norfolk, being led and seduced by the Devil … hath lately, within the King's own court and mansion-palace at Westminster … without the knowledge or assent of our said most dread Sovereign the King, contemptuously and traitorously contracted himself by crafty, fair and flattering words to and with the Lady Margaret Douglas, being natural daughter to the Queen of Scots, eldest sister to our said Sovereign Lord, by which it is vehemently to be suspected that the said Lord Thomas falsely, craftily, and treacherously, hath imagined and compassed – that in case our said Sovereign Lord should die without heirs of his body (which God defend) then, that the said Lord Thomas, by reason of marriage in so high a blood … should aspire by her to the imperial crown of the realm, or at the least making division for the same. By all likelihoods, having a firm hope and trust that the subjects of this realm would incline and bear affection to the said Lady Margaret Douglas, being born in this realm, and not to the King of Scots her brother, to whom this realm hath nor ever had any affection.[1]

A private Act of Parliament, to which Henry attached his own assent, ruled: 'That the offence shall be judged and deemed high treason, and that Thomas Howard might be attainted of high treason, and suffer such pains and execution of death to all intents and purposes as in cases of high treason.'[2]

Satisfied that he had then made Thomas Howard an example of what could be expected by anyone aspiring to advance themselves by marriage to a person even distantly connected to the Tudor dynasty, Henry then sanctioned the passing of yet another statute by which it became high treason for anyone to marry or seduce any lady related to the royal blood. The penalty for doing so being that whoever attempted it would be:

... deemed a traitor to the King and his realm, and with his abettors shall suffer the pains of execution and death, loss of privilege and sanctuary, and forfeiture of lands and hereditaments to all intents as in the cases of high treason ... And be it enacted that the Woman (after the last day of this Parliament) so offending, being within the degrees so specified, shall incur like danger and penalty as is before limited and shall suffer such-like death and punishment as appointed to the Man offending.[3]

Margaret, although secretly petrified, as she certainly must have been, nonetheless managed to maintain her dignity and hide her feelings, much as can be imagined, to the chagrin of the uncle, who was bent on destroying the spirit of his once favourite niece. Overwhelmed by all that was happening to her, she became extremely ill, and that Henry did have some feeling for her is shown by his sending first his apothecary, Thomas Aske, 'with certain medicines for her use' and then, on these failing to show any improvement, his own doctor, a man named Cromer. It must have been some satisfaction to Margaret to learn that these visits cost £14 6s 4d, a sum which Henry himself was forced to pay.

The illness from which Margaret suffered is said to have been 'Tower Fever'; this was in fact malaria, then common in the south east of England, particularly in the damp district of the Fens, from whence it inevitably spread to London, carried by the many travellers and merchants who frequented the city. It seems to have been highly infectious within the confinement of the Tower, because Thomas Howard soon sickened with it, to Margaret's great fear and concern. Although supposed to have no communication with each other, the lovers smuggled letters and poems by means of gaolers or servants, who conveyed them in secret ways. Margaret wrote to Thomas:

I may well say with joyful heart,
As never woman might say before,
That I have taken to my part
The faithfullest lover that was ever born.

Great pains he suffers for my sake
Continually night and day

For all the pains that he does take
From me his love will not decay.

With threatening great has he been paid
Of pain and eke of punishment,
Yet all fear aside he has laid:
To love me best was his content.

Thomas, and one supposes Margaret, are known to have been much influenced by Thomas Wyatt, the lyrical poet who was the first to write sonnets in England. Wyatt, an exceptionally tall and handsome man, who had first entered Henry's service in 1516, was suspected of being one of Anne Boleyn's lovers, for which reason he had also been imprisoned in the Tower very shortly before her execution. Known to have been a friend and great admirer of Henry Howard, Earl of Surrey, himself a poet of some fame, he may have had some access, again by surreptitious means, to Surrey's younger half-brother, Thomas, who now, in his bouts of fever, was scarcely able to write.

10

BARGAINING COUNTERS OF THE KING

Meanwhile, in Scotland, the news of Margaret's cruel and manifestly unjust imprisonment did at least invoke, to some extent, the sympathy and anger of her mother. It was now eighteen years since Queen Margaret had even seen her daughter, let alone contributed towards her welfare. Despite protests to her father that he would not return her 'for our comfort', she would seem to have banished her from her mind. Now, when she had parted from her third husband, the man she had created Lord Methven, contemptuously referred to by Henry as Lord Muffin, she suddenly became solicitous for the daughter she had virtually abandoned. Her renewed maternal affection, however, barely concealed her wish for her brother to invite her to England.

On 12 August, from Perth, she wrote to Henry, strongly reproaching him for his cruelty and imprisonment of her daughter and Thomas Howard, whose betrothal he had first encouraged, which she knew that he could not deny. Demanding that her daughter be sent back to Scotland, she assured him that should this happen she would never trouble him again. Henry did not reply, and later she was to claim that his treatment of Margaret had made her so angry that she had actually forsworn her intention of visiting her brother and of remarrying Margaret's father, the Earl of Angus, whom she knew to be at his court.

Henry, for his part, had no sympathy for her marital problems, despite their similarity to his own. He had better uses for Angus than to see him once again united to the sister, whose fickle mind he distrusted, as by now he had good reason for so doing. He would certainly not allow Margaret Douglas to return to Scotland, it being all too obvious that once there she could become a political pawn to be used against him, as her mother must well have known.

Ironically, it proved to be fortunate for Margaret that her uncle refused to let her leave England, where, at least, she was comparatively safe. In Scotland, her half-brother, King James, was furious that her father Angus had given allegiance to Henry; while unable to punish him in person, he was venting his anger to all those connected with him, in particular his sister Janet.

Janet, who had married firstly John Lyon, Lord Glamis, and then on his death Archibald Campbell of Skipness, was arrested for the crime of witchcraft on the orders of the king. Together with her second husband, she was imprisoned in the dreadful dungeons of Edinburgh Castle, from which, no doubt by bribing the jailers, he managed to escape, while she was left incarcerated to face a terrible death. James was merciless. Some of her relations and servants were tortured until they screamed out confessions, which were enough to convict her of the crime of sorcery of which she was accused. In July 1537, she was burned at the stake on the esplanade of the castle, her young son being forced to watch her dreadful death.

Incarcerated in the Tower since the month of July, Margaret, Henry was suddenly informed by the keeper, had become dangerously ill. The former intermittent fever had returned.

The king was placed in a predicament: he did not want to release Margaret but neither did he want her to die. Therefore he ordered Thomas Cromwell, his Lord of the Privy Seal, to request Agnes Jourdan, the abbess of the magnificent abbey of Sion (which, because of its usefulness for female prisoners, he had not attempted to destroy) to accommodate the Lady Margaret Douglas and her servants for as long as should be required.

The abbess replied from Sion on 6 November, to the effect that 'As touching the Lady Margaret Douglas' she would be glad to receive her 'to such lodging, walks, and commodities as may be to her comfort', but she did ask that someone 'such as you do trust and think apt' might be sent to make the decision as to which part of the building would be 'most convenient for the purpose'. This being complied with, Margaret, it would seem, was allowed to leave the Tower in the second week of November.

Once installed in Sion Abbey, in its beautiful site above where the branches of willows reached down towards the Thames, Margaret had a degree of the freedom she had lacked so greatly in the Tower. Walking between the ancient mulberry trees overhanging garden paths, she could at least take some exercise and regain the strength of her limbs. And even in the damp mists above the river, she could breathe in country air. Always she thought of Thomas, first as she once had known him, a young man full of life and the love of riding, jousting in the lists at full tilt; then, from what her servants told her from gossip with others they had met, she thought of him lying thin and consumed with fever in a cell, which in the months of winter was hardly warmer than the ice-bound streets outside.

It was not long before those servants of Thomas' brought her yet further news. Their master, they said, was dying. The fever had turned into consumption. He could not have long to live. As for themselves, they were starving. Thomas had no money and the keeper, apparently acting on the king's orders, refused to feed them in the Tower. Margaret said she would lodge them and, as in the parable of the loaves and fishes, they could share her own servants' food.

This, while to her seeming reasonable – it was all she could do to help Thomas now so ill and alone – was not viewed as such by the abbess, Agnes Jourdan, with whom Margaret was now on bad terms. The abbess, in all fairness, would seem to have had some reason why such charity should not be given. Margaret's servants at this period, from her own description, seem to have been largely men. Amongst them were her chaplain, a gentleman 'that guarded her chamber', plus another gentleman and the groom of her wardrobe, who is thought to have been Peter, he so dextrous with his needle, who mended his lady's gowns. In addition she appears to have had visitors, or so Agnes Jourdan claimed; if this was true, it must have meant much extra provisioning at a time when, due to bad harvests, there is known to have been a shortage of food.

Complaints were made to Cromwell by the abbess, who told him that, in addition, Margaret was giving shelter to Thomas Howard's servants as a means of keeping in touch with him in the Tower. Henry, predictably furious when told of this by his Lord Privy Seal, immediately ordered him to write to Margaret, berating her of her generosity, inevitably at his own expense, and again listing the offences of which she had been charged. Then, surprisingly, and to her it must have seemed almost miraculously, he informed her that the king had promised to restore her to favour if she would renounce her betrothal to Thomas Howard, still held on a charge of treason for his presumption in trying to make her his wife.

Margaret's spirit was broken: her defiance was at an end. Her uncle had achieved his object in making her obedient to his will. Knowing that however much she loved him, she could now never marry Thomas, she longed only to regain the freedom that towards the end of her imprisonment she had thought she would never achieve. In proof of her contrition, deeply as it must have hurt her pride, she replied to Cromwell, swearing obedience to her uncle. Also, in denial of all the rumours which she knew he must have heard, she affirmed that she was still virgin, so that, according to her own word, her supposed marriage had not been consummated, even if it had actually taken place.

My Lord

What cause have I to give you thanks, and how much bound am I unto you, that by your means hath gotten me, as I trusted, the King's grace and favour again. Besides that it pleaseth you to write and give me knowledge wherein I might earn his Grace's displeasure again, which I pray unto the Lord to sooner send me death than that. I assure you, my Lord, I will never do that thing willingly that should offend his Grace.

And my Lord, whereas it is informed you that I do share the house with greater numbers than is convenient, I assure you that I have but two more than I had at the Court, which were indeed Lord Thomas' servants. The cause I took them for was for the poverty I saw them in, and for no cause else. But seeing, my Lord, that it is your pleasure that I shall keep none that did belong to my Lord Thomas, I will put them from me. And I beseech you not to think that any fancy doth remain in me touching him, but that all my study and care is how to please the King's Grace and to continue in his favour.

And, my Lord, whereas it your pleasure that I shall keep but few here with me, I trust you will think that I can have no fewer than I have; for I have but a gentleman and a groom that keeps my apparel, and another that keeps my chamber, and a chaplain that was with me always in the Court.

Now my Lord, I beseech you that I shall know your pleasure, if you would that I should keep fewer. Howbeit, my Lord, the servants have put the house to small charge, for they have nothing but the remains of my board, nor do I call for nothing but that which is given me, however I am very well entreated.

And, my Lord, as for resort, I promise you I have none, except it be gentlemen that cometh to see me, nor never had sin I came thither. If any resort of men had come, it would neither have become me to have seen them nor have kept them company, being a maid as I am.

Now, my Lord, I beseech you to be so good as to get my poor servants their wages, and thus I pray our Lord to preserve you, both soul and body.

By her that has her trust in you.

Margaret Douglas.'[1]

Whether or not he believed Margaret to be as contrite as she claimed, Henry allowed her freedom as part of the general rejoicing when, on 12 October 1537, his longed for son, Prince Edward, was born. Queen Margaret, up in Scotland, writing to Lord Herbert of Cherbury on the 30th of the month, told him that 'it was a comfort to hear that her daughter had been released from the Tower'.[2]

Amazingly, she does not appear to have realised either that Margaret's very severe illness had been the reason for this happening or that, for the space of nearly a year, she had been held again in custody at Sion Abbey.

Margaret may have been freed from there, or was on the point of departure, when, on 31 October, the day after her mother's letter had been written, she was told that Thomas Howard had died.

Historians are in agreement that his death was caused by illness brought on by his close confinement and almost total lack of exercise. His nephew, the Earl of Surrey, swore that he had died for the loss of Margaret, with whom he had been so greatly in love.

Thomas, who had written so many poems to Margaret while they were both in prison, sending her words of promise of the future they would now never share, finally wrote his epitaph as he knew he was soon to die.

For you yourself doth know,
It is not long ago,
Sith for his love one of our race

Did end his life in woe.
In Tower both strong and high,
For his assured truth,
Wherein with tears he spent his breath,
Alas, the more the truth!

Thomas' mother, the Dowager Duchess of Norfolk, begged the king to be allowed to bury her son. Henry replied through Edward, brother of the queen, who he had had just made Earl of Hertford; he, in turn, informed Thomas Cromwell of what the king had decreed.

My Lord

I have showed the King's highness of my Lord Thomas' death, as master Wriothesley desired me, as also my lady his mother's request for the burying of him. His Grace is content she hath him according to your advice, so that she bury him without pomp.[3]

Thus, in obedience with the king's orders, Thomas Howard was buried by his mother. Probably buried at night by the light of a lantern, he lies in some quiet corner, where a stone laid to his memory, if ever there was one, has long since disappeared.

11

The Second Lady In The Land

The birth of Henry's longed for son, Prince Edward, changed Margaret's proximity to the throne. Now that she was no longer heir apparent, the king, in the magnanimous mood which followed the birth of his son, restored her to court favour as, through her mother, his sister, she became the second lady in the land.

Then, when Queen Jane died of puerperal fever just ten days after the birth of the prince, Margaret's station was again elevated above that of both of his daughters, now declared illegitimate, by his previous wives.

Margaret herself was hardly aware of this and cared less even if she knew. Only four days before she had been told of the death of Thomas Howard, and now she was ordered by Henry to ride from Hampton Court to Windsor in the funeral procession of the recently deceased Queen Jane.

Her feelings can only be imagined, as dressed in deepest black, she rode on a palfrey, specially trained to carry a side saddle, with trappings of the same colour of mourning, led by her squire behind the cortege. Depressed and miserable, her face mercifully hidden behind a black veil, her sorrow was only lessened by the presence of Princess Mary, who, restored to her father's favour through the influence of Queen Jane, was now chosen by him as chief mourner as his wife was carried to her grave. Behind, in a carriage pulled by horses draped in black, came their cousin Frances, eldest daughter of the Queen Duchess Mary, as the Duchess of Suffolk had been known. Frances, who had much of the beauty of her mother, the aunt whom both of her nieces had both so greatly loved, was now the Marchioness of Dorset and herself the mother of a son.

Queen Jane was buried in St George's chapel, Windsor, where later, at his express wish, her husband King Henry was to lie beside her, the acknowledged favourite of his wives.

The court was dull that summer of 1538. Not only was it in mourning but England was in a state of crisis, threatened with invasion from the combined armies of Austria, Spain and France.

The Catholic countries of Western Europe had united, threatening Protestant England: the King of France, Francis I, having come to terms with the Holy Roman Emperor, Charles V. Taking advantage of their alliance, the Pope had sent his ambassador, Cardinal Pole, son of Lady Salisbury, to persuade the emperor to invade England. Theirs would be a Catholic crusade against King Henry, whose excommunication three years earlier had not yet come into effect.

Henry reacted to the threat by imprisoning leading Catholic families: Cardinal Pole's relations being special targets for revenge. Firstly, in August 1538, his brother Geoffrey Pole was arrested and sent to the Tower. Questioned, probably with torture, he revealed family secrets which led to the arrest of his older brothers, Lord Montague, whose son disappeared in the Tower aged 12, and the Marquess of Exeter, held a state prisoner together with his wife and a young son.

Most dreadful of all was the treatment of old Lady Salisbury, once venerated by Henry to the point where he had made her both godmother and guardian of his daughter Mary. Held under house arrest for a year, she was then, at the age of 70, sent to the Tower, where, not allowed even warm clothes and bedding, she suffered misery from the cold.

Margaret, in this instance, was thankfully spared the dreaded punishment of prison walls. Henry was fond of his pretty niece who, so Cromwell had told him, was now entirely subdued to his will. But she was a Catholic, as obdurate in her religion as his daughter Mary. As such she was a danger to the succession should anything happen to his one, rather delicate son.

Over the years his spies had reported to him that some people in Scotland maintained that the marriage of Margaret's parents had been illegal at the time of her birth. Initially Henry had taken these rumours to be inventions of enemies, particularly those of Margaret's father, the Earl of Angus, long denounced as a traitor in Scotland for accepting Henry's pension in return for fighting for his cause. However, were her parent's marriage proved to be unlawful, Margaret, as illegitimate, could no longer be a claimant to the throne.

The man sent as Henry's ambassador specifically to investigate the legality of his sister's marriage to the Earl of Angus was none other than Princess Mary's chamberlain, William Howard, an elder half-brother of Thomas, the lover, if not secret husband of Queen Margaret's daughter and namesake, the niece who the king now wanted to disown.

William returned from Scotland with the news that Henry wanted to hear. Some of those questioned had assured him that the marriage was questionably valid. Angus had previously been betrothed to Janet Stewart, daughter of Lord Maxwell of Traquair, the long-time mistress to whom during his marriage to Queen Margaret he had frequently returned. The incident of how he had deserted his wife when she had fled to England with her baby daughter was clearly remembered. Where else had Angus gone but back to his mistress?

All this gave Henry the evidence that he needed to exclude Margaret in the line of inheritance, making it certain that on his death a Protestant should inherit his crown.

Margaret is known to have lived with Princess Mary and Princess Elizabeth, now 4 years old, either at Hunsdon or Beaulieu for a period of some months. She was certainly at Beaulieu in June 1538 when she gave Princess Mary 20s, either as a present or repayment for a debt, both being gamblers at cards.

At the following Christmas, spent that year at Westminster Palace, Margaret won a frontlet, or ornamental border to a headdress, from Mary, which had cost her 20s, as is proved by the expenses of her Privy Purse. From the same evidence, it emerges that Mary gave a mark to Margaret's chaplain, a man named Charles, and the same to her grooms at New Year.

It was Princess Mary who, on the orders of her father, had to break it to Margaret that she had now been declared illegitimate. Perhaps the depth of their friendship softened the blow; whatever Margaret's reaction to

12

THE FLEMISH WIFE

Deputising for Princess Mary, who was ill once again, Margaret was sent to meet the king's bride. Together with her other cousin Frances, the Marchioness of Dorset, she rode at the head of a procession of eighty-five court ladies to receive the German princess. The rendezvous was the mound near the cross at Blackheath, near to what was then the high road, where, on the king's orders, were erected tents of gold cloth.

All of the welcoming party waited in excitement to see the beauty whose portrait, painted by Holbein, had so greatly entranced the king. But as the horses of her carriage were reined in so that Anne of Cleves could step down, there were muffled gasps of disappointment. This apparently middle-aged lady (she was actually only 24), despite being slim and fairly tall, had dark hair and a swarthy skin. Moreover, instead of smiling, she looked not only apprehensive but severe. Nonetheless, nodding her head to acknowledge their greeting, unsure of how to reply in the language she was trying so assiduously to learn, she kissed both Margaret and Frances, before all the other court ladies were presented to her in turn.

It was then Margaret's duty to ride at the head of the procession that followed the king and his bride, whose unattractive appearance had been such a shock to him at first sight, from Blackheath Cross to Greenwich Palace.

Here, despite his outspoken misgivings, on 6 January 1540, Henry married Anne of Cleves.

A month later, on 4 February, the king took his new wife from Greenwich to Westminster to present her to the city as previously he had done with Jane. Barges, magnificently decorated, were rowed in procession up the river. The first held the king, a huge, unmistakeable figure, who none on the banks could fail to recognise if only on account of his size. 'Bluff King Hal' to his cheering people, he came with his consort of nobles, picked by right of birth from the highest in the land. Behind followed the queen and her household, with Margaret, also distinguished by her height and the red hair falling on the shoulders of her velvet cloak, taking pride of place. The Londoners, loving such a spectacle, shouted, sang and danced with joy. Cannons roared from the Tower 'with a sound like thunder' as the procession passed by. Finally, on reaching Westminster, the queen, followed by her ladies, was armed ashore.[1]

Henry's marriage to Anne had been suggested by Cromwell, who saw it as a diplomatic move to counter the ongoing threat of an invasion by the allied armies of France and the Holy Roman Empire. The danger had seemed more imminent when it was believed that the king and emperor were preparing to sign a treaty with the Schmalkaldic League. This alliance 'of all Protestant princes and free cities', comprising seven princes and eleven cities, of which Dusseldorf was the capital, dated from 1530. Then the formidable block of states, bishoprics and duchies, stretching as far north as the Baltic, had been formed with the prime object of curbing the aggrandisement of the Emperor Charles, territorial ruler of the Netherlands.

Duke John of State of Cleves, which was included in the Protestant League, had already proposed a marriage between his heir, William, and Henry's daughter Mary, a suggestion repudiated on the grounds of her religion. But Duke John had four daughters and Cromwell, seeing the great advantage to England of forestalling a possible alliance of France and Austria with the Schmalkaldic League, had told Henry that one of them, named Anna, 'excelleth as far the Duchess [of Saxony, her sister] as the golden sun excelleth the silver moon'.[2]

Unbeknown to him, in doing so, he had signed his own death warrant. Repulsed by the physical appearance of Anne of Cleves, Henry was soon to be made aware that, as far as political advancement was concerned, he need never have married her at all.

In the spring of 1540, the alliance between King Francis and the Emperor Charles broke up in a prelude to ensuing war. Thus Henry had married the wife he disliked for no political gain. Who was to blame but Thomas Cromwell? Henry, who had just created him Earl of Essex, now made Norfolk his instrument in bringing about his end. Cromwell, the blacksmith's son who had made a fortune in money lending before becoming Wolsey's man, now had few friends left in either the government or the Church. On 10 June, when Norfolk accused him of treachery, the whole assembled council endorsed the charge. Denied a trial, he was executed in the Tower on 28 July.

13

THE ROSE WITH
MANY THORNS

The king's brief marriage, never consummated, proved to be little more than a farce. Within weeks he had focussed his attention on one of her young ladies-in-waiting, none other than the niece of his second wife Anne Boleyn, a plump and pretty girl named Catherine Howard, aged only 17. Margaret probably knew of her reputation. Growing up in her grandmother's household, she had already become compromised, both with the music teacher, a man named Henry Madox, and her grandmother's secretary, Francis Dereham. Nonetheless, despite her tarnished reputation, her uncle, the Duke of Norfolk, had procured her a place at court.

Innocent as he seems to have been of her character, Henry was soon totally in love with the girl he called 'his rose without a thorn'. Within months he was giving her presents, mostly length after length of velvet and cloth of gold. Totally besotted, he married her just weeks after the annulment of his marriage to Anne of Cleves.

On the same day, 28 July 1540, Thomas Cromwell – Henry's chief minister for eight years, his strongest advocate for the Reformation of the English Church and the man behind the annulment of his first marriage, so recently created Earl of Essex in reward – was beheaded on the block on Tower Hill.

Cromwell's death was a salutary warning of how, under Henry's despotic power, even the mightiest could fall. No one was more aware of this than Margaret, now high in his favour but always in fear of what might happen should her uncle find fault. Once again made first lady, she was given a suite of rooms in Hampton Court. She is known to have been at Reading Palace, on her way to take up her appointment, on 22 August 1540.

A list of the allotments of the apartments at Hampton Court shows those of the Lady Margaret to have been at the foot of the stairs leading to the Queen's Gallery. She must have felt a personal connection with the palace if only because it had been built by her godfather, Cardinal Wolsey, determined to show that the king's chief minister could live as graciously as any cardinal in Rome. Wolsey had given it to Henry in a last, desperate effort to be restored to favour, when knowing he stood on the cusp of disgrace. Henry, determined to make the palace a showpiece of his power, had set to work to make it large enough to hold most of the near thousand people who at that time attended his court. Having extended the vast kitchens, he had set to work on the Great Hall, with its intricate hammer-beam roof, with such impatience that the masons had been forced to work by candlelight throughout the night. Now, with his masterpiece completed, he dined on a raised dais above the assembled company below.

Most original of all the king's innovations was the post-Copernican astronomical clock, which, at the time of Margaret's arrival, had just been erected on the gatehouse of the second inner court. Considered one of the wonders of the world, it showed not only the time of day but the phases of the moon, the month, the quarter of the year, the date, the sun and star sign; most marvellous of all, the clock showed the high water at London Bridge, where at low tide the surging current made it dangerous to travel up the Thames to London by boat.

There was much entertainment in the great new palace where the young men could amuse themselves by playing tennis on the newly built courts. Also, its very size, with its many stairs and corridors, was an inducement for illicit meetings, particularly after dark. Soon it was being remarked upon that Queen Katherine, who loved dancing and entertainment, never seemed to go to bed. Later it was to transpire that some of her clandestine meetings had been with Frances Dereham, her grandmother's former secretary, who, given the fact that he was known to have been her previous lover, she most unwisely employed. Also her name was being linked to a dashing young man called Thomas Culpeper, who, as a gentleman of the privy chamber, was familiar with and popular with the king. It soon leaked out that Katherine's accomplice in her assignations was a foolish woman called Lady Rochester, whose husband, Anne Boleyn's brother, had been executed for supposed incest with his sister, an accusation never proved.

Margaret, who must have been aware of the insinuations and whisperings that were going on, probably chose to ignore them, being herself involved in a love affair. The queen's brother, Charles Howard, thanks to his sister's influence, had been given a post at court. Good looking, like most of the Howards, Margaret, who herself at twenty-five was at the height of her beauty, fell in love with him and he with her.

Their romance, although encouraged by Katherine, was once again forbidden by the king, who fearing that both she and his daughter Mary might be used as figureheads should a Catholic rising break out again in the north, sent them both under house arrest to Sion. Fortunately, the former abbess, Agnes Jourdan, who had quarrelled with Margaret over what she had claimed was her extravagance, had been replaced by an apparently more amenable lady called Clementia Tresham.

It must also have been some consolation to her that Charles Howard, unlike his unfortunate cousin Thomas, was spared punishment. This must have been, at least in part, due to Henry's continuing infatuation with his young wife, Charles' sister Katherine, who in the early part of the summer of 1541 made a tour with him in the north of England. The reason for this 'progress', as it was termed, was that in April there had been further dissension in Yorkshire; here, five years earlier, the country had been torn apart in the rebellion which had begun as the peaceful demonstration known as The Pilgrimage of Grace.

Henry had now become paranoid in his fear of a Catholic rising. Convinced of a national rebellion on the scale of civil war, he ordered that the Tower be cleared of state prisoners to be ready to house the rebels who would soon be brought in chains.

But this in itself was not enough. Still obsessed with loathing for Cardinal Pole, who had sent him his published treatise the *Pro Ecclesiasticae Unitatis Defensione* in which he openly denounced his policies, he ordered the execution of Pole's mother, the saintly Lady Salisbury.

This was she whom the king's daughter Mary regarded as a surrogate mother. Likewise, his niece Margaret Lennox, even if once constrained by her strictness, remembered with deep gratitude the kindness with which she had been received at Beaulieu, where she had arrived, almost as a vagrant, eleven years ago. Neither she nor Mary could save her, knowing full well that even an approach to Henry could only result in punishment, perhaps even death for themselves. Like others who greatly pitied her – scandalised that an old lady of 70, known to be innocent, should suffer in such a way – they had to wait helpless while the sentence of death was carried out.

It proved to be particularly horrible, a young executioner, untrained to his task, literally hacking her to death. Buried in the chapel of St Peer ad Vincula within the Tower, she was venerated by the Church of Rome.

She was not the only one to die.

14

THE FALL FROM GRACE

The queen was still in great favour with Henry when they returned to Hampton Court in the autumn of 1541. But by now she had made many enemies, particularly through installing her friends and relations in much coveted positions at court. Amongst them was John Lassells, a fervent Protestant, who believed that through her influence over Henry she was doing the devil's work. Lassells had a sister, Mary, married to a man named Hall, who had been a servant in the Duchess of Norfolk's household at Lambeth; Hall told him, in no uncertain language, how Katherine had behaved at that time.

It was not until 2 November that the fateful day occurred. As they attended an All Souls' Day mass, Archbishop Cranmer gave Henry a letter informing him that, on the sworn word of a chambermaid in her grandmother's household, Francis Dereham had once been not only Katherine's lover but had also openly called her his wife.

Henry, furiously disbelieving such slander, as he then thought it to be, nonetheless allowed Cranmer to investigate; forthwith, both Dereham and Culpeper, to whom Katherine had written a love letter in her very distinctive hand, were dragged off to the Tower. Questioned under torture, they admitted that they had had some sort of dalliance with the queen but swore that sexual intercourse had never taken place. Nonetheless, it was enough to condemn her. Charged with treason, she denied infidelity but admitted that before her marriage she had behaved with impropriety on more than one occasion.

Margaret and Mary at Sion must then have heard the pathetic story of how Katherine, although constantly watched, had somehow managed to reach the Royal Chapel, adjacent to her rooms, where she knew Henry to be attending mass. Hammering on the door, she had screamed for him to help her until the guards had dragged her away. Even Cranmer pitied her, saying that it would touch any man's heart to witness her distress. But Henry, remorseless as he had been to Lady Salisbury and to Katherine's aunt and predecessor, Anne Boleyn, ordered that she would be imprisoned at Sion, from whence his niece and daughter had to be removed.

Prior to her departure, Margaret was harangued by no less a person that Cranmer himself, who lectured her, on the instructions of Sir Ralph Sadler, who for his part had been told by King Henry to deal with his 'troublesome womankind'. Told that she had behaved indiscreetly, first with the Lord Thomas and then with his cousin Charles Howard, she was warned 'to beware the third time, and wholly apply herself to please the King's Majesty'.[1]

Margaret, with the awful example of the fate of Catherine Howard still upmost in her mind, listened demurely to his lecturing, terrified, as she must have been, that this was only a preliminary to further imprisonment or death.

Waiting in such fear that it is doubtful if she could sleep at night, she eventually heard, to her enormous relief, that this time it was not the Tower but the Duke of Norfolk's house in Norfolk, Kenninghall, where she was to be sent on 13 November. With her went the former Mary Howard, now the Duchess of Richmond, young widow of Henry's illegitimate son by his mistress Bessie Blount, who had died aged only 17. Sir Ralph Saddler, put in charge of the operations, wrote:

The King's pleasure is, that my Lady Mary be conducted to my Lord Prince's house, Havering Bower, by Sir John Dudley, with a convenient number of the Queen's servants; and my Lady Margaret Douglas to be conducted to Kenninghall, my Lord of Norfolk's house in Norfolk, in whose company shall go my Lady of Richmond, if my Lord her father and she be so contented.[2]

Why, under the circumstances, Margaret was sent to be the ward of the uncle of the man whom Henry had refused to allow her to marry is extremely hard to comprehend. It can only be presumed that Henry was afraid of antagonising Norfolk, magnate of the north of England and thus essential to his rule. Since the arrest and trial of Norfolk's niece was known to be imminent, perhaps Henry sent Margaret into his custody as a means of keeping his good will. Significantly, if Charles Howard escaped disgrace for his temerity in wishing to marry Margaret, Henry, in pardoning him, must have done so for good reason.

Kenninghall, a derivation of King's Hall, had been given by Henry to Thomas, the second Duke of Norfolk, who had pulled down the old house to build a palace in its place. Margaret was here when she heard that her mother had died at Methven Castle, home of the third husband she had been doing her best to divorce. Margaret, who had only dim memories of the woman from whom her father had taken her when she was only 3 years old, if saddened, can hardly have been surprised. Sir Ralph Sadler, sent to Scotland by Henry to negotiate with James V in the previous year of 1540, had reported on his return that Queen Margaret was both broken in spirit and infirm in health. Finding that her brother had not even written to her, she had told him rather pathetically, 'Though I be forgotten in England never shall I forget England.'

Yet, despite her despondence, this still formidable woman had continued to connive at politics. Now at odds with her son and his powerful wife Mary of Lorraine, she had written to her 'dearest brother' in her own handwriting on 12 May 1541. Telling him to 'write nothing concerning me, your sister, to the King my son', without first consulting her and asking her advice. Also she had begged him 'to keep secret any writings that I send, for otherwise it may do me great hurt'.

Queen Margaret had been struck with palsy [the word then used for a stroke]. At first it had not seemed serious but as she grew worse a message was sent to her son, King James, at his hunting lodge of Falkland Palace. Summoning confessors, she instructed them most urgently 'to sit on their knees before the King, her son, and beseech that he would be good and gracious to Lord Angus'. Likewise they were to beg him to 'be good to the Lady Margaret Douglas, her daughter, and that he would give her what goods he had left, thinking it right because her daughter had never had anything of her'. Most emphatically, she insisted before them, that Margaret had been born during her marriage to Angus and therefore was undeniably legitimate. She died on 18 October 1541.

15

THE LENNOX
EARLDOM RESTORED

On the news of his sister's death, Henry immediately sent a courier to his Berwick herald, a man named Harry Ray, telling him to go to Scotland to find out if she had left any property in England and to enquire into how and why she had died. Ray returned with the news that Henry must have expected: Margaret had left no property in England. Her cash box, when opened, had proved to hold 1,200 marks, but her jewels, which she had so specifically bequeathed to the daughter whom she had neglected as she had confessed, had been largely seized as Scottish heirlooms by her son and his French wife.

Most importantly, however, the priests, who as confessors had heard Margaret's last words, told Ray that her daughter was without question legitimate. This sworn testimony now could never be denied.

Margaret herself was forced to realise that under the present circumstances, with war between Scotland and England just about to break out again, asking her brother to return the jewels bequeathed to her could only be a waste of time. She is believed to have been in Norfolk when her father, Archibald Earl of Angus, suggested that she should marry Patrick Hepburn, Earl of Bothwell, outlawed from Scotland like himself.

Margaret, in this instance, agreed to the idea, but nothing came of it for reasons unexplained.

Shortly, Angus was ordered to command part of Henry's army, under Sir Robert Bowes, in an attack on the Scots. Margaret, who must have seen him fairly frequently while he and she were both at court, now said 'good-bye' to him for what proved to be a very long time.

Once into the Border country, in August 1542, the English army was defeated at Haddon Rig by James' commander, the Earl of Huntly. After the battle, Angus, while retreating, nearly lost his life as a Scottish soldier, throwing a rope round his neck, all but pulled him from his horse. Gasping against its throttling pressure, he somehow managed to draw his dagger, hack through the suffocating cord and escape. But Henry, furious when told what had happened, gave him no sympathy and merely railed at his defeat.

King James, delighted, went so far as to offer the hand of his sister Margaret to Huntly, his victorious commander. Margaret, however, refused any such suggestion, furious that her brother had had the audacity to describe her as his base sister, inferring that she was illegitimate. In any case, the idea of marriage to Huntly quickly vanished as James, accusing him of being dilatory in not pursuing the English following their defeat, dismissed him from command of the army. In his place he appointed the Earl of Moray, who promised him that further action would be taken 'before this moon is out'.[1]

The king, together with Moray and Cardinal Beaton, then advanced into Dumfriesshire with an army estimated at nearly 20,000 strong; James, with part of his force, remained at Lochmaben, waiting to cross the sands of Solway at low tide. Oliver Sinclair, in command of the rest of the army since the forfeiture of Angus the keeper of Tantallon, then took a more eastern route. Confronted by Thomas Wharton, the English warden of the Borders, near the river Esk Sinclair, the king was totally defeated: his army driven back to destruction on the Solway Moss.

Plunged into one of the fits of depression from which he habitually suffered, the king made his way to Hallshill, Fife; here Lady Kirkaldy of Grange did her best to assuage his misery as he told her he would be dead within fifteen days. Her son William, a boy of 14, was with the king when he died at Falkland Palace on 14 December 1542.

Margaret can hardly have grieved for her half brother: after the three years that he had been her father's ward when they had both been very young, she had never seen him. She is known to have spent Christmas that year at Hundson near Ware in Hertfordshire, with her cousin Princess Mary, to whom she gave a gown of carnation satin as a New Year's present. The gown was stitched up in the latest Venetian style by the ever-industrious Peter, who received 20s for his work.

Soon afterwards she must have heard the exciting news from Scotland, where, following the king's death, a political revolution occurred.

On 29 December some of the Scottish prisoners taken at Solway were released. Henry, however, granted them freedom at a cost. They were forced to pledge their assistance towards the betrothal of the newly born Mary Queen of Scots to his son Prince Edward, now a little boy of 5. In addition to this, no less than ten of them swore under pressure to accept Henry as King of Scotland in the event of the young queen's death. Likewise, the Earl of Angus, an outlaw since 1528, together with George, his brother, and another exile the Earl of Bothwell, were commissioned to return to Scotland on the orders of the English king.

On 13 March the Scottish Parliament rescinded the forfeiture of Angus and the other former outcasts and restored them to their lands. At the same time the governor, James Hamilton, Earl of Arran, was acknowledged as next in line to the Scottish throne. Commissioners were then appointed to arrange a future marriage between the infant queen and Henry's son.

Meanwhile the French king, Francis I, was just as eager as Henry to send exiles home to Scotland to advance his own cause. Amongst them was Matthew Earl of Lennox, eldest of the three boys who had been sent to France following the murder of their father, treacherously killed by James Hamilton while attempting to rescue King James V at Linlithgow Bridge in 1526.

Lennox, through his descent, was in fact more French than Scottish. The line of Darnley Stewart had long been naturalised in France, the name being changed to Stuart in accordance with French pronunciation. His great grandfather, a member of the famous Garde Écossaise, the bodyguard of the kings of France, had been made Lord D'Aubigny by King Charles VII. Defending Joan of Arc, he had died gallantly in 1429. Matthew's father, John Stuart of Darnley, had returned to Scotland in 1495 to become a great favourite of James IV, who had restored him to much of the ancient Earldom of Lennox; this included Stirlingshire, parts of Perthshire and Renfrewshire and the whole of Dunbartonshire. Subsequently, on John Stuart's marriage to Lady Jane Hamilton, a sister of the Earl of Arran and granddaughter of James II, King James had confirmed his right to the Earldom of Lennox, which had been recreated for his grandfather in 1488.

Matthew Lennox himself had fought with distinction in the Italian wars of Francis I. An officer in the Garde Écossaise, he cut a dashing figure with his height and striking good looks. Enticed originally to Scotland by Cardinal Beaton, on the suggestion that he marry the widowed Mary of Lorraine, he had left France with the promise of both military support and money by King Francis. Returning in the greatest secrecy, he had come ashore in Scotland at his own castle of Dumbarton, perched on a rock at the mouth of the River Clyde. From there, after riding across Scotland, he is known to have been with the queen mother, Mary of Lorraine, at Linlithgow Palace on 5 April 1543.

Brought up in France, this young man of 26, with much natural charm, had been schooled in the sophistication of the French court. For Mary of Lorraine, it was as a gift from heaven to be able to converse in her own language and to hear so much news from home. Matthew for a time courted her, until it became obvious that, much as she liked him, she did not wish to marry again.

Meanwhile Henry VIII, having heard of his arrival, began to make his own plans. His niece Margaret was 28, and although still so striking in appearance that many called her beautiful, she would soon be beyond marriageable age. Henry now devised a way of making use of her to further his own aims. Forthwith his ambassador to Scotland, Sir Ralph Sadler, was instructed to sound out Lennox on the idea of marriage to Lady Margaret Douglas. Since her father's pardon by the Scottish Government, she was now heiress to his estates. Lennox, when approached, seemed agreeable to the suggestion. However, Sadler confessed to King Henry that he did not know what to make of him, guessing, quite rightly, that he was waiting for a better offer from the King of France and meanwhile sitting on the fence.

Three months after Matthew Lennox had arrived in Scotland, on 12 July 1543, King Henry VIII had married his sixth wife, the clever and sensible Catherine Parr, under whose calming influence he had decided to be reconciled to his daughter Mary and likewise to Margaret, his niece.

Margaret was summoned to Hampton Court to be one of the bridesmaids at her uncle's wedding.

Almost immediately afterwards Princess Mary became gravely ill. Thin to the point of emaciation as she already was, she had succumbed to a fever which reduced her almost to a wraith. Margaret rushed to join her and the two of them, with Princess Elizabeth, by now a little girl of 5, went to the Palace of Ampthill in Bedfordshire.

This was the castle built in the previous century by Sir John Cornwall, whose wife Elizabeth was the sister of Henry IV. King Henry VIII had acquired it in 1524, and Mary's mother, Catherine of Aragon, had been held there during her divorce proceedings in 1533. For this reason it had an unhappy ambience for Mary. The companionship of Margaret was, nonetheless, a consolation, and while there, the ever useful Peter embroidered a pair of sleeves for her with which she was so delighted that he was given 7s 6d. Soon afterwards, Mary, in return, gave Margaret £4.

Princess Mary recovered and she, together with Margaret and the little Princess Elizabeth, joined the new Queen Catherine at Westminster Palace that Christmas of 1543. Mary, presumably in gratitude for all they had done to help her during her illness, gave Margaret's three women three gold sovereigns and her men-servants twenty shillings.[2]

Meanwhile, in Scotland, the struggle for power between Mary of Lorraine, the Queen Dowager, and the Regent Arran continued with unabated strength. On 9 September 1543 the coronation of the little Queen Mary, then barely a year old, took place in Stirling Castle. Lennox, having taken part in the ceremony, hurried to his stronghold in Dumbarton where French ships were due to arrive. On 5 October, they sailed into the Clyde to anchor by Dumbarton Rock. With them came the promised money, with which Matthew was supposed to raise a force in Scotland to detract Henry's army from France. Matthew, however, having given the French captain a receipt for it, kept the money in Dumbarton Castle specifically for his own use.

16

THE PRICE PAID
FOR A BRIDE

On 11 December the Scottish parliament denounced the treaties with England and confirmed its allegiance to France. This proved a pivotal reason for Matthew Lennox to align himself to the pro English party, which, on the outskirts of Edinburgh, had assembled a large army at Leith.

Cardinal Beaton, who held the office of chancellor, foremost amongst the Francophiles, is believed to have put forward an over ingenious scheme by which the ongoing feud between the Hamiltons and the Lennoxes might be brought to an end. Arran would be divorced and would then marry Mary of Lorraine, while Matthew Lennox, although twenty-five years her senior, would be wedded to the little queen and thereafter become lieutenant-governor. Subsequently, on 13 January 1544 Margaret's father, Archibald, Earl of Angus, and Matthew Lennox, enemies as they had once been now pledged themselves to loyalty both to the queen and to Arran, still the nominal regent, in defence of the Church and the realm.[1]

However, the enmity between Matthew Lennox and James Hamilton, Earl of Arran, was still far from subdued. Lennox, using the money, arms and ammunition which had been sent from France, took control of

Glasgow and Paisley, which lay within his own domains. Joined by the Earl of Glencairn, and supported by the MacFarlanes, his vassals on Loch Lomond, he was narrowly defeated by the regent's army in a battle on Glasgow Muir. Besieged then by Arran in Glasgow, he eventually had to surrender but retired to the safety of Dumbarton Castle with its escape route to the sea.

He sailed from Dumbarton in the spring of 1544, but once off the shore of north-west England, he landed at Chester, from where he made his way overland to Carlisle. There, by arrangement, he met Henry's delegate, Lord Wharton, deputy-warden of the English marches, who dictated King Henry's terms. Assembled with Matthew were his brother, Robert, now the Bishop of Caithness, and Thomas Bishop, the secretary whose sinister presence ever dogged his steps. Also present were two Cunninghams: Hugh and William, the latter the Earl of Glencairn, who, in return for his promise to deliver Dumbarton Castle to the king, was given 1,000 crowns.

Matthew Lennox pledged himself to surrender, not only Dumbarton but also Rothesay Castle; of much greater significance, he also promised to do all in his power to prevent the young Queen Mary from being sent to France. Instead he would carry her over the border to the English king. Upon this being accomplished, Henry guaranteed to make him Lord Governor of Scotland while, in the meantime, repeating the offer of the hand of his niece, the Lady Margaret Douglas, together with the promise of a yearly pension of 500 English marks.

Lennox, thus tempted, finally made the decision to throw in his lot with England rather than the King of France. Leaving his brother as hostage for his commitment, he once more went aboard at Chester and made full sail for the Thames.

Meanwhile, in London, the old palace of St James, newly redecorated by the king, was alive with noise and excitement as preparations for Margaret's wedding began. Most active of all, in getting the servants to scurry about, cleaning and polishing and arranging tables and chairs, was the Princess Mary, who herself remaining unmarried, rejoiced at what she prayed would be the future happiness of her cousin and dearest friend.

But how did Margaret herself feel about being used as a bargaining chip by her uncle to achieve his political ends? Henry appeared to be oblivious to the fact that since Matthew's father had been murdered by James

Hamilton at Linlithgow on the order of Margaret's father, Angus, the families involved had been irreparably estranged. Many people pitied her for being forced to marry the son of her father's victim who, despite her own innocence, must surely bear her ill will.

Margaret herself must have been apprehensive if not actually terrified of the life that lay before her with a man who was not only her father's enemy but, having left Scotland as a boy, reputedly entirely French. It must also have been extremely hurtful to know that her prospective bridegroom had wooed her sister-in-law, Mary of Lorraine, before, on her rejection, submitting to her uncle's bribery.

Matthew Lennox had reached London by the 26 June as is evident from the marriage contract, drawn up on that date. It detailed Margaret's future husband's lands in Scotland, which were to be her dower. Matthew himself dictated the Gaelic names to the English clerk, whose spelling leaves much to be desired. First in the lands of the Lennox itself were Glenrinne, Balloch and Arthinturless. Then, even more difficult to decipher, in the Lordship of Darnley in Renfrewshire, the baronies of Chukispe, Ynchchilune and Craig of Nielstown. Lastly, in Perthshire, all the lands of Erere (Earn?) of the annual value of 5,000 marks. Matthew, in appending his signature to the above, signed himself 'Matthew, Orle of Levinax ...'

Most magnificent of Margaret's wedding presents were those given by Princess Mary, who, in her jewel inventory, kept by a lady called Mary Finch, described the details of her gifts.

A balas ruby, with a diamond table cut, set over it like a glass, with several middle sized pearls pendant from the same. Another large balas ruby, and a diamond, with one great pearl – but the diamond was taken out to set in a girdle buckle. A brooch of gold with a large sapphire: a brooch of gold with a George of diamonds. A brooch of gold with a balas ruby, and the History of Susanne, painted in miniature. Likewise others with the history of David, of Noah's flood, set around with many rubies and diamonds, and finally one with the history of our Saviour, healing the man with the palsy, which was a table diamond set in the gold embossing.[2]

The evidence of the date, subscribed on Margaret's dower lands, suggests that she had barely a fortnight to get to know her bridegroom before their marriage took place. The results of their meeting seem to have been favourable. Tall and handsome, with the exquisite manners he had learnt at the French court, Matthew was far from the ogre she had pictured in her mind. Being much the same age – Matthew, born in 1516, was just a year younger than she – they certainly made a handsome couple. Even George Buchanan, John Knox's biographer and tutor of James VI, usually sparing with his praise, describes her as 'a princess renowned for the beauty and comeliness of her person' while Matthew's 'valour, his beauty, his lofty stature, and skill in all martial exercises had rendered him one of the most admired cavaliers in France'.[3]

King Henry, evidently delighted at so successfully disposing of his niece to his own benefit, was munificent in his reward to her bridegroom who had so conveniently acceded to his will. In return for Matthew's surrender of both Dumbarton and Rothesay castles, he gave him property in England valued at an annual rate of £1,700 sterling.

These were the lands of Temple Newsam, near Leeds, which had recently fallen into his hands by the forfeiture of Lord D'Arcy and Meynel, one of the leaders of the Pilgrimage of Grace. Henry himself dictated the letters of naturalisation for both Matthew and his secretary, Thomas Bishop, on the 6 July 1544.

This was the day when Margaret and Matthew were married in the chapel of St James's Palace. The ceremony was conducted with all the pageantry and colour so dear to the Tudor heart. The women wore square-necked dresses with v-shaped waists and embroidered sleeves, the skirts spread out over panniers, called farthingales, to give a regal effect. Probably, it being summer, the materials were satin and silk. The fashion for brides to wear virginal white being not then in existence, Margaret, it is fair to imagine, wore a gown and train of the much prized cloth of gold.

King Henry attended the wedding together with his queen, Catherine Parr, his daughter Mary and probably, as Margaret had been head of her household, the little red-haired Elizabeth. A wedding feast followed the ceremony when minstrels played and wine flowed.

By marrying Margaret, Matthew, already in line to the Scottish throne, was now in place to the English succession, as well did her uncle know. The monarch, raising a toast to his niece, then famously and publicly declared that in the case of his own children failing to succeed him, he would be 'right glad if heirs of Margaret's body succeeded to the crown'.[4]

The feasting over, the jollity continued as the couple, treated like royalty, were publicly put to bed. At least in this instance they were adults instead of, as happened so frequently, being hardly of consenting age. Margaret and Matthew, although still virtually strangers, found each other so conjugal that rapidly they fell in love.

Their newfound happiness, however, was short lasting, for only a few days later, Henry, with the army withdrawn from Scotland, embarked for France. Matthew, following his orders, with the 500 men who could be spared, then took part in a naval expedition sailing to the west coast of Scotland.

17

'Every Day Like Sunday'

On 8 August 1544 King Henry, by then in France, made Matthew Lennox his lieutenant for the north of England and for southern Scotland where an English army, under the Earl of Hertford, had already caused ruthless devastation during the summer months.

Matthew, in the meantime, was aboard an English vessel, which was part of a naval expedition sent to harry Scotland's west coast. On 10 August he landed at Dumbarton Castle, where, expecting to be welcomed into his own fortress, he instead nearly lost his life. He was actually in the chapel, explaining his contract with King Henry, when the captain of the castle, suddenly drawing his sword, called him a traitor and demanded his immediate surrender to the Scottish government. Matthew, astounded, barely understood the man's words, but his secretary, Thomas Bishop, standing by his side as usual, had the presence of mind to seize a pair of pikes from the wall.

Thrusting one into Matthew's hands, the pair of them, their armour protecting them against the most vicious blows, fought their way out of the castle and to the boat lying against the steps below. Waiting at the ready, the oarsmen pulled out to the warship lying in deeper water off the castle rock, where, once aboard, the loaded cannons were enough to put off pursuit.

Seizing the chance of rebellion against the governor and the council, a consortium of Highland chiefs formed a 'rebel council'. It included the Macleans of Duart and Lochbuie; the MacLeods of Harris and Lewis; MacKinnon of Strathardle; MacNeil of Barra; MacIan of Ardnmurchan; Clanranald, chief of South Uist; and Donald Dhu MacDonald, in *de factum* the last Lord of the Isles.

From the mouth of the Clyde, the fleet of galleys, carrying the Highland warriors – fierce, bearded men, armed with axes and awesome claymores – sailed south through the Brennan Sound. Guided by the jagged mountain of Goat Fell, landmark of the Island of Arran, they landed on the Hamilton's island to raid and burn the little farming villages, plundering all they could find.

Next, after pillaging Bute, they headed back to Argyll to continue their marauding campaign along the coast. Then, as a scout reported the approach of sails on the skyline, they put out to sea to intercept some French ships returning from an expedition from Newfoundland to France.

Tom Bishop, sent to report these proceedings to the English king, sailed over to France where Henry had just taken Boulogne. Henry, ecstatic with his own success, reportedly received him with open arms, but, told of Matthew's failure to take Dumbarton, he expletively expressed his anger, denouncing him as incompetent for failing to achieve an easy task.

As all this was happening, Margaret remained at the court of Queen Catherine, made regent during Henry's absence in France. No two women could have been more different than the last of her uncle's wives. Whereas Catherine Howard had been plump and small, Catherine Parr was as tall as Margaret. Catherine Howard had been pretty. Catherine Parr, if not exactly ugly, was plain.

The difference did not end with their appearance. Catherine Howard, wilful and capricious as a child, had been self-centred, whereas Henry's new wife, childless despite two previous marriages, was a mother figure who drew his family together under her protective wing.

'Her rare goodness made every day like Sunday, a thing hitherto unheard of in royal palaces,' wrote Francis Goldsmith, her chaplain. Writing to her from France in his own hand, King Henry added the postscript, 'Give in our name our hearty blessings to all our children.'[1]

It was largely thanks to Catherine's influence that, by special act of parliament, the illegitimacy of both Mary and Elizabeth was revoked. Mary, now again entitled princess, was to remain in her household throughout her reign as queen.

Queen Catherine was more nurse than wife to her husband, now grossly overweight. She made many potions herself to try and heal the ulcer in his leg from which he suffered greatly. Although not a beauty, she was possessed of great elegance, the only thing that she had in common with her predecessor being that she loved dancing and beautiful clothes.

On 17 February 1544 the Spanish Duke of Najera, special envoy to the Emperor Charles V, arrived at court. The king was ill but the queen and Princess Mary, to whom he was conducted by Eustace Chapuys, the Spanish ambassador to England, graciously received him. The duke's secretary, Pedro de Gant, left an engaging description of a ball at which he was a guest.

Catherine looked regally magnificent in a gown of rich crimson and cloth of gold with a golden girdle and a train two yards long. Round her neck she wore two crucifixes and a jewel set with magnificent diamonds while other stones sparkled in her headdress.

After the duke had kissed the queen's hand, she led him into another room, where he was entertained for several hours with music and much beautiful dancing. Although the queen herself was feeling unwell, she danced most beautifully with her brother, William Parr, now made Earl of Essex, the title of Thomas Cromwell, recreated by the king. All eyes then switched to watch the small dark figure of Princess Mary, in cloth of gold and purple velvet, as she partnered the tall, red-haired Lady Margaret Douglas, also beautifully attired.

Mary, obviously in vivacious form, then paired up with some gentlemen of the court, one of whom, a Venetian, danced galliards 'with such extraordinary activity that he seemed to have wings on his feet. As the evening drew to a close, the queen summoned a Spanish-speaking nobleman to present her gifts to the duke, then rose and offered Najera her hand to kiss. He would have kissed that of the Princess Mary but she offered her lips and so he saluted her and all the other ladies.'

Obviously this was an evening that the Spanish secretary, for one, would never afterwards forget!

18

SADNESS UNFORESEEN

Despite his anger with Matthew, Margaret was still in favour with her uncle; even with his preoccupation with matters of state, Henry asked frequently after the well-being of his now pregnant niece. Ironically, this most unpredictable of men, who had thrown Margaret in prison for falling in love with a man not of his choice, seems to have had genuine affection for his niece, perhaps because her height and red hair that was so very Tudor in appearance or because he recognised in her a spirit as staunch as his own. Nonetheless, even if flattered by his enquiries for her, Margaret was always aware that her true value to her uncle was that of her renewed importance as a bargaining counter in his dealings with the recalcitrant Scots.

There is no evidence whatever that Henry, despite his avaricious nature, constrained by the rules of consanguinity, made amorous advances to Margaret himself; the fact that she remained in his fickle favour suggests that since her politically convenient marriage, arranged so adroitly by himself, he had recognised that the only daughter of his sister should be given the status due to her close proximity in line to the throne.

This seems to have been the main reason why, either during his absence or after his return from France, King Henry allowed her to live in Stepney Palace. And it was here in February 1545 that her first child, a son whom she tactfully named after Henry, was born.

Again Princess Mary, so much happier than before, was delighted. As her jewel inventory proves, she sent Margaret a lace of goldsmith's work set with little sparks of diamonds and rubies and twenty-one pearls to ornament her son's christening robe. The child was certainly born healthy, but, sadly, as happened so frequently at that time due to lack of medical knowledge, he did not survive infancy. The little boy, Henry, Lord Darnley, the first to bear that name, died when he was only 9 months old. He was buried at the end of the chancel at St Dunstan's church in Stepney. A brass plaque with an inscription placed above the pathetic little grave was inscribed with the words:

Here lieth Henry Stuart Lord Darnley, at the age of three quarters of a year, late son and heir to Matthew, Earl of Lennox, and the Lady Margaret his wife, which Henry deceased the twenty-eighth day of November, in the year of God 1545, whose soul Jesus pardon.

The sorrow of his parents was intense, made more so because, having been forced by circumstances to leave him when he was only a few months old, neither was beside him when he died. Little Henry had been left at Stepney as a hostage to ensure his parent's fealty while their fortunes were once more plunged into jeopardy. His maternal grandfather, Angus, infuriated by the destruction of Douglas graves at Jedburgh, having turned his coat to give his allegiance to Scotland, had defeated the English army at Ancrum in the same February that little Henry Darnley was born.

King Henry planned a reprisal, intending to send an army of an estimated 36,000 men both overland and by sea to overwhelm the country he was determined to annexe to his own in a yet unprecedented show of strength.

The Scots, aware of the threat they faced, assembled a large army within the space of under a year. The attack came in September as Edward Seymour, the Earl of Hertford, made another devastating war of aggression on the Border lands south of Edinburgh, burning everything in his path. At the same time Matthew Lennox, joined by Highland clans, rebellious to the government, was causing yet more destruction in the islands of Bute and Arran, and on the west coast of Argyll.

Margaret, in his absence, had been away from London when their baby died because she had gone north to Yorkshire to take control of the lands of Temple Newsam in the West Riding, granted to them by Henry in the previous year. Included in his bequest were the domains of Jerveaulx Abbey, once one of the most important churches in Yorkshire but now, since the desecration of the monasteries, merely a magnificent shell. The Cistercian monks had long vanished. The only relic of their order being the name of the last Abbot, Adam Sedbar, scratched on the wall of his cell in the Tower of London when imprisoned there for heresy in 1537.

But at Temple Newsam, where the knights of the Order of the Temple had also long been gone, all was bustle and commotion as Margaret began setting the house, vacant since the forfeiture of the family of Lord D'Arcy, into a home once more. It was here at Temple Newsam that her second son, Henry Stuart, Lord Darnley, named after the elder brother who had died just three months before, was born on 7 December 1545.

The baby, when only a few months old, was put into the care of a reliable middle-aged man named William Taylor, chosen by Margaret because of his Catholic religion, who was to stay with Henry throughout his life. Little could Taylor, when accepting his prestigious appointment, have foreseen the horrendous circumstances under which he would die for his loyalty, together with his precious charge.

In trusting him with the care of her little son, Margaret knew that she could rely on Taylor at a time when she was fighting against the jealousy of Tom Bishop, that enigmatic man, described as her husband's secretary, who seems to have had a hold over Matthew for reasons which are largely obscure.

The corps of his ongoing feud with Margaret seems to have been that of religion. Margaret, a devoted Catholic, was struggling to make Matthew adhere to her creed, while Bishop, a Protestant, urged him continually to accept the reformed religion as a means of furthering his influence over the English king. Why Margaret tolerated Bishop in her household is an unexplained mystery. Presumably, having come from France with Matthew, he was an old retainer. However, in his letter to Cecil describing the fracas at Dumbarton Castle, he makes derogatory remarks about his employer, implying he showed cowardice as they fled, at Matthew's instigation, beating off their attackers with pikes in their ungainly retreat to the sea.

That Margaret failed to get rid of him proved nearly fatal for her. Once installed in Yorkshire where the Catholic religion prevailed, Bishop, seething with resentment at feeling himself isolated amongst enemies, became an English spy. Lurking in corners and behind tapestries covering the walls, he listened to private conversations between Margaret and Matthew; he reported what was said in letters, somehow smuggled to William Cecil, the clever young lawyer who under the protection of Edward Somerset, brother of the late Queen Jane, was able to pass on their contents to King Henry.

Consumed with his hatred of Margaret, Bishop wrote that she was encouraging her husband to correspond with certain of the king's enemies in Scotland. On receiving this information Henry became, as Bishop had rightly predicted, almost insane with rage. Determined to punish her for what he saw as wilful betrayal, her uncle, now a very sick man and often confused in his mind, decided to change his will. Despite what he had said in that jovial speech at her wedding, he now demoted her in the rights of succession. By declaring that the descendants of his younger sister Mary, the Duchess of Suffolk, should supersede those of his elder sister Margaret, lately the Queen of Scotland, he robbed Margaret, the niece he had once acknowledged as the second lady in England, of her rightful place in the line of accession to his throne.

Margaret and Matthew, knowing this and realising the danger in which they stood, can only have been greatly relieved when they heard that on 28 January 1547 Henry VIII, whose gross obesity is thought to have been the cause of his suffering from type two diabetes, had died in his Palace of Whitehall.

19

'Let a Trumpet be blown on the marches'

Taking their 2-year-old son with them, the Lennoxes made their way south to make their obeisance to the young King Edward VI. The difference between the two boys was most noticeable. Despite being eight years younger than Edward, Henry Darnley was a strong child, exceptionally tall for his age. Edward, in contrast, although the son of a gigantic father, was unnaturally pale and thin.

The Lennoxes had many good connections. Matthew was a close friend of Robert Dudley, son of the all-powerful Northumberland. He was also companion-in-arms to Edward Seymour, the former Earl of Hertford, now made Duke of Somerset, who, in the young king's minority, had become Protector of the Realm. Yet despite knowing men of such influence, the Lennoxes, on arrival both at Hampton Court and St James's Palace, were very coldly received.

Chagrined by the antipathy shown to them by the new regime, they returned to Temple Newsam, thankful at least that the house, parkland and farms were still in their possession, as surely they would not have been had King Henry remained alive.

From there, in the following September, Matthew had no alternative other than to prove his obedience to the new young king by raising a force to fight in Scotland, under Somerset's command. Margaret, as Tom Bishop certainly suggested in his reports to Cecil, must have had divided loyalties in the 'War of the Rough Wooing', as this conflict came to be known. She could hardly have had otherwise. Angus, her father, now pardoned by the Scottish government, would be fighting against her husband in the forthcoming campaign.

Torn between love for the husband, to whom she was devoted, as all contemporaries relate, and filial affection for her father, hero of her early years, Margaret faced the dilemma with commendable common sense. To have refused Somerset's order would have meant imprisonment or worse; even if spared the punishment of being sent to the Tower, she and Matthew would have lost Temple Newsam, where the land produced not only their income and sustenance for their large household but also provided some stability as the only real home that they possessed.

The Scottish ambassador in London, Sir Adam Otterburn, sent urgent messages to the Regent Arran in Scotland warning him of the preparations for war. Early in September 1547 an army was marching north from England. Reinforced with several hundred German mercenaries, and a large contingent of cavalry, it reputedly numbered 16,000 men. Behind them came the siege engines, cannons of deadly force, dragged by teams of horses and oxen on creaking timber frames with iron wheels. Moreover, there was another threat: the great cavalcade was supported by a fleet of warships from the sea.

Once across the Border, Somerset shared command with Lord Dacre. Their combined force then advanced up the coast of East Lothian, keeping in touch with the ships sailing for the mouth of the Forth. Ahead of them, just south of Musselburgh, the Governor Arran, with the main part of the Scottish army, said to number about 22,000 men, waited on the west bank of the River Esk, aiming to stop their approach. On the left was the Firth of Forth, on the right, a very large bog.

On the morning of 10 September, Arran moved his army over a bridge across the Esk. The infantry was commanded by Angus, while Arran himself, together with Huntly, led the vanguard. The commanders are said to have been in disagreement: one cause of the fiasco which occurred. As the left wing of the army came under fire from the English ships, the panicking men of the vanguard pushed into the central division, causing great confusion. At the same time, on the right wing, Somerset's cavalry blocked all attempts at advance. The Scottish army was penned in between the River Esk and the sea without room to manoeuvre and unable to return enemy fire. Slaughtered from three directions, by guns and a hail of arrows, it was forced to retreat in what became a disastrous rout. Many men drowned in the Esk, trying to swim across. Others were mown down by archers and pikemen as they tried to escape through the bog.

Margaret's father, the Earl of Angus, was amongst those who survived. Made prisoner, he was taken to Drumlanrig to be placed under house arrest.

20

THE HOSTAGES

Following his victory at Pinkie Heugh, Somerset stationed the English army at Haddington in East Lothian. From there, while still threatening the capital city of Edinburgh, he could control the Firth of Forth. Such was the lack of authority in Scotland that some of the landowners in the south part of the country, believing that the marriage of their queen to King Edward would accrue them some benefit, actually transferred their loyalty to the English.

The master of Maxwell was one of the Border landlords who treated with the English. In order to free his father, Lord Maxwell, from imprisonment in the Tower, he had some time previously promised the English ambassador, Sir Ralph Sadler, that he would do his utmost to serve his country's interests in Scotland. Subsequently however, the Governor Arran and the Lords of the Scottish Council had compelled him to give security by keeping his castles of Caerlaverock, Lochmaben and Threave for the queen 'from their enemies of England'. Thus, inadvertently, he was caught between both sides, as was to prove disastrous for him when the test of conflicting loyalties took place.

On 27 January 1548 the Earl of Arran, still officially the governor, bribed by the promise of the French Duchy of Châtelhérault, promised that he would secure the consent of the Scottish parliament to the marriage of their queen and the dauphin. In proof of his word, the fortresses of Blackness and Dunbar were given to the French who installed garrisons forthwith.

In February 1548, commanding a section of the army, Matthew Lennox and deputy warden of the English Marches Thomas Lord Wharton marched west to Dumfries to destroy the town of Annan, which they took after a heroic defence. Wharton had been promised the support of 2,000 men by the Master of Maxwell, who, in confirmation of his intentions, had left hostages, sons of the local Border lairds, in the royal castle of Carlisle. However, on reaching Carlisle with Wharton, Matthew Lennox found that Maxwell had reneged on his word. Whereupon, obsessed with fury at his deceitfulness, he ordered the young hostages to be hanged.

Accounts of the time are conflicting, both as to the number of hostages and to how many were actually killed. The nineteenth-century historian Agnes Strickland, quoting Lord Herries' Memoirs, claimed that eleven out of twelve were executed while only the young son of the Master of Maxwell, thanks to the kindness of a soldier who could not bear to pull the rope round his neck, was spared. Caroline Bingham, however, in her excellent biography of Darnley, says that a court was convened to decide their fate, after which only four out of ten were killed while the remaining six were reprieved.

Whatever the true story, it does seem possible that Tom Bishop, Matthew's secretary, a man who appears to have had an almost Machiavellian influence over him, may have urged him into the action which he afterwards lived so bitterly to regret. Bishop's correspondence with Cecil is revealing. In one letter, he actually boasts that:

> Above all others my countrymen, I have been most earnest, most inventive, most cruel, most careful to subvert that realm of Scotland. Let a trumpet be blown on the Marches, requiring any of that nation or of France to come forward to charge me, I seek not Scots to try my doings, but noblemen of England under which I serve.[1]

Can it be that Matthew – who, as is known, was easily influenced both by his wife and his secretary – succumbed to the suggestion that he needed to show a heavy hand and committed an atrocity that afterwards never left his mind?

Later, Margaret, describing his bouts of depression, was to claim that he suffered from 'a disease which solitariness is most against'. From this it has been taken that his guilt over ordering the deaths of young boys, some hardly older than his own son, was the cause of the mental anguish which plagued him for the rest of his life.

The disastrous defeat of the Scots at Pinkie Heugh accelerated the struggle between the French and English to win control of Scotland. The Governor Arran persisted in his liaison with the French King Henry II, who succeeded his father Francis I in 1547, to try to get aid from France.

In the uncertain situation, the government in Scotland, lacking firm leadership, was virtually out of control. The English were at the gates of Edinburgh, threatening to storm the city. At Stirling, the queen mother, Mary of Lorraine, was terrified that her little daughter, Mary Queen of Scots, would be seized and carried across the Border. She sent her to the Island of Inchmahome, on the Lake of Menteith, where she stayed for six weeks until it was thought to be safe enough for her to rejoin her mother in the strongly fortified, almost unassailable, castle of Stirling.

Then, in June 1548, in answer to Arran's supplications, a French force landed at Leith. The Scottish army, with French reinforcements, attempted to relieve the besieged town of Haddington; here, on 7 July, in a nunnery nearby, an agreement was signed promising Mary Queen of Scots as a bride to the Dauphin of France.

The French galleys, having landed their troops, then sailed on from Leith. They travelled round the north coast of Scotland and down the west to Dumbarton, where, at the end of July, the little queen and her four Marys were taken aboard to sail for France. The winds were fair: the flotilla, having rounded the north coast of Ireland, landed safely near Brest. Six months later, in February 1549, in recognition for his part in organising the marriage between the Scottish queen and the dauphin, Arran was rewarded with the French duchy of Châtelhérault.

21

'MY DERREST DOUCHTER'

In the spring of 1548, previous to the little queen's escape, Matthew
Lennox and Lord Wharton, after causing much destruction and leaving
its ancient church in ruins, left the town of Annan. They then moved on
to Drumlanrig, where, in the fourteenth-century castle of the Douglasses,
Matthew's father-in-law, Angus, had been held after being taken prisoner at
Pinkie Heugh. Angus had written to them from the castle to ask what they
meant to do with him, to which they had promptly replied, 'They be only
favourable to those who favoured the godly marriage [that of Mary Queen of
Scots and Edward VI] and peace.' However, by the time they reached the
castle, which they then proceeded to destroy, Angus had somehow managed
to escape. From Edinburgh he reached the Highlands by sea, returning
only to Tantallon when the hunt for escaped prisoners had died down.

He was certainly in his castle in the summer of 1548, because
Margaret, having ridden from Yorkshire to join her husband, probably in
Dumfriesshire, sent him word that she wished to see him and was bluntly
told not to come.

There is good reason to believe that it was fear of Matthew Lennox which
made Angus refuse to see his daughter in such an unfeeling way. He was all
too aware that since his return to Scotland Matthew, holding him responsible for his father's death, had nursed his relentless hatred. Margaret,

nonetheless, was furious as well as deeply hurt by her father's cruel rebuff, for which probably, at least in some part, she blamed his new young wife.

Following his divorce from her mother Queen Joan, Angus had at first returned to his mistress, Janet Stewart of the Dumfriesshire family of Traquair. It would appear to have been after Janet's death that he had married Margaret Stewart, daughter of the 5th Lord Maxwell of Traquair, the man who had reneged on Matthew Lennox, causing him to hang the young hostages at Carlisle. This second marriage, to a girl who must have been younger than his daughter, had resulted in the birth of two young sons.

Margaret, therefore, formerly his heiress, was now deprived of her inheritance by the births of these two young boys. Thought to have been so near to Tantallon that she could actually see the massive fortress on the rock-bound coast, she realised with great bitterness that she was now expelled by her father from her childhood home.

Under these circumstances, it is even more extraordinary that hardly was she back in Yorkshire before a messenger from her father appeared on a sweat-covered horse. Opening the letter which the messenger pulled from his saddlebag, she found to her amazement that it came from her father, who now had the temerity to beg her to help their relations, held prisoner, as he claimed, and in great danger of their lives.

Another fortress taken by the English army was the even more ancient castle of Dalkeith where Margaret when not at Tantallon, had spent part of her early years. The men of the Douglas family taken prisoner and sent to the Tower were, Angus claimed, in great distress and poverty.

It seems hardly credible, that after so many years of neglecting her, he now had the audacity to write to his daughter asking her to provide for these men and give them the protection of taking them into her house. Typically, he made no secret of the fact that he cared more for his nephew, married to an heiress, than he did for his own illegitimate son whose mother was his longterm mistress Janet Stewart of Traquair.

Derrest Dochter

After my maist tender recommendations and hearty blissing, this sal be to advertise you, that through mischance and under traist as I believe, the house of Dalkeith was ditroyit. And taken furth it our cousin the Laird of Glenbervie, the Master of Morton, George my son, David Home of

Wodderburne, and Alexander Home his eme [uncle]. Praying you, with advise of your husband to se gif ye can get them, or part of them, put in friend's hands, and gently treated there, and specially the Laird of Glenbervie, that is ane sickly tender man, and has ix motherless bairns; and let George lie in pledge for him, as zour wisdom thinks best. And make my hearty commendations to my Lord, zour husband, and give credence to this bearer, my servitor, David Stewart, as to myself, and God preserve you.

Written at Edinburgh the xx of June 1548.

Zour father,

Ard Earl of Angus

To my derrest Douchter, the Countess of Levenax.[1]

Margaret was at this point living at Temple Hirst, originally one of the preceptorys of the Order of the Knights Templar, which, in 1308, had been sequestered by the Sheriff of Yorkshire on the king's writ. Since then, the house, with its 200 acres, had been part of the Temple Newsam estate.

On receiving the letter she consulted her husband, just returned from Scotland, who in turn talked it over with the messenger, David Stewart, who was able to give him details of the state to which the Douglasses were reduced.

The Lennoxes faced a dilemma. While Margaret, having been a refugee herself, knew how her relations were placed, common sense warned that in helping them, she would be putting not only herself but also Matthew and their immediate family into a situation of great danger. Matthew, on the other hand, while aware of the risk he was running in playing a double game, saw that with the support of the Douglasses, he might regain his forfeited Scottish estates.

Deciding to play for safety, Matthew wrote to Somerset, with whom he was on friendly terms after soldiering with him in Scotland. He enclosed both Angus' letter to Margaret and one from Angus' brother, Sir George Douglas of Pittendreich, with a short explanation of his own. Referring to Margaret's uncle, he told Somerset that he had required his niece to ask 'that his grace will permit her (if he will not grant the keeping of all the Douglas prisoners) to take home his son, the Master of Morton, as well as the sick Laird of Glenbervie'.

Matthew then added, sarcastically, that it was evident that Sir George Douglas cared more for his younger son, husband of the heiress to the earldom of Morton, than he did for the elder, who he had offered to leave as a hostage in prison. So much did his father value the younger son (albeit that the Morton heiress was mad) that he had actually written to Matthew to say that there was no limit to the amount of money that he was willing to pay for a ransom and neither would he exchange him for 'any English prisoner the Scotch had in their hands'. Lennox wrote the following, with some bitterness:

> The Earl of Anguish [*sic*] might better have dressed [addressed] themselves to others to have been suitors for them than either my wife or me, for we have received no such benefit at nother of their hands so to do, but rather to desire to keep them fast when you have them, like as always my poor opinion has been … Notwithstanding, if it shall please your Grace that I may have the keeping of the Master of Morton and the Laird of Glenbervie with the others, I shall answer for the sure keeping of them always to your Grace, for I would be very glad to prove what fruit might follow the fair words of the Earl and his brother.[2]

Thus did Matthew make it clear to Edward Somerset that in helping his wife's relations, he expected something in return. Still playing for safety, he added a postcript. 'My wife hath desired me to make her humble recommendations unto your Grace and saith that she will make answer neither to father nor uncle until she know your Grace's pleasure therein.'

Then sending off this missile with a fast riding messenger, he labelled it 'Haste – post haste – haste with all possible diligence.'[3]

Somerset, in reply, agreed to the suggestion that the Douglasses could be freed from prison if Matthew and Margaret were willing to be responsible for their keep. Subsequently, they opened their doors at Wrexham Castle to what would have seemed a strange collection of people: the old and obviously dying Laird of Glenbervie, with, one must presume, his gaggle of nine motherless children. Their arrival must have reminded Margaret of her own at Berwick, when Lord Strangeways, reluctant as herself at that moment, had been forced to lower the drawbridge to allow a 15-year-old vagrant and her equally destitute attendants to enter the safety of the castle.

The family of Glenbervie did not come alone. With them were two other Douglas relations: James, Master of Morton, and Margaret's own illegitimate half-brother, George. Both were arrogant young men, entirely devoid of compunction in the exploitation of anyone who might restrict their devious ambitions.

James, Earl of Morton, Margaret's first cousin, was the son of Angus' ruthless brother George Douglas. By marrying Elizabeth, the heiress of her father the Earl of Morton, James had become the Master of Morton (courtesy title of a peer's eldest son). The fact that Elizabeth, like both of her sisters, was mentally deficient, had done nothing to deter either James or his father from achieving such an affluent and influential match.

Despite her mistrust of her relations, Margaret could not have known, or even guessed, how one day these young men to whom she was giving sanctuary were to be so disastrously involved with her own son, Henry, at that time just a year old.

As she watched with great pride, the fair haired, sturdy little boy, so noticeably tall for his age, taking his first unsteady steps, not a vestige of intuition warned her that by agreeing to her father's request to harbour indigent relations, she was sheltering the very men whose daggers would one day take his life.

22

THE FALCONER
MESSENGERS

Matthew Lennox had been granted land in Yorkshire, surrendered to the Crown by the sixth Earl of Northumberland following his family's involvement in the Pilgrimage of Grace. In addition to this Matthew had been made castellan, or governor, of Wressil Castle near Stamford Bridge in the East Riding, where he and Margaret kept up what can only be described as a provincial court.

Wressil Castle, built between 1380–90 by Sir Henry Percy, Earl of Worcester, in the time of Richard II, was renowned as one of the most magnificent houses north of the Trent. A quadrangle building with five towers, one at each corner and a fifth over the gateway, it was surrounded by two moats, within which lay a terraced formal garden.

In addition to land in Yorkshire, the Lennoxes also received the Percy residence at Hackney near London. This was of course most useful when both had periods of attendance at the young King Edward's court. In the absence of a queen, however, ladies-in-waiting were redundant; Margaret, who with a growing family was finding it increasingly difficult to combine the roles of mother to her children and servitude to a monarch, was given leave to abandon her position and retire to her Yorkshire home.

The family's main base was Temple Newsam, core of the widespread estates. From there, as then was customary, she moved her household to the other houses of Temple Hirst and Wressil Castle for the purpose of collecting rents and using the farm produce with which much of them were paid. Also, when not in occupation, the vacant houses were cleaned from top to bottom, a process which, with so many occupants, was essential at the time.

It would seem that the Douglas visitors, who must have arrived in the late autumn of 1548, were still ensconced in one of the Lennox houses in Yorkshire, most probably Wressil Castle, when, on 16 February of the following year, Margaret had another letter from her father, to tell of the deaths of his two baby sons. He gave no reason as to what had killed them, but it is known that the winter that year was exceptionally cold, so only the slightest infection could have developed into something serious as the ice cold wind from the North Sea howled through cracks in Tantallon's ancient walls.

Now once again his heiress, Margaret replied to her father's letter, not, as he might have expected, with commiseration but instead in a renewed tirade against his treatment of her in the past. Heading her missive 'the King Majesty's Castle of Wressil', and dating it 15 March 1549, she told him, in no uncertain terms, what she thought both of him and of and his brother George, whom she strongly suspected, with reason, of being after the inheritance which was once again hers.

My Lord

After my humble commendations, and desiring of your blessing, this shall be to signify to you the great unnaturalness which you show me daily, being too long to rehearse at all points, but some I will declare.

Now the worst of all, my Lord, is that, being near you, and most desirous to have spoken with you, yet you refused it, and would not, wherein you showed yourself not so loving as you ought to be, or else so unstable that anyone may turn you. For divers times you have said you would be glad to speak with your son. [Matthew Lennox]

My Lord, remember he hath married your own daughter, and the best child to you that you ever had, if you call to mind your being here in England. Howbeit, your deeds show the forgetfulness thereof, insomuch that you are so contrary to the King's Majesty's affairs that now is, his father being so good and so liberal a prince to you, which ought never to be forgotten.

But now my Lord, I hear say that you have protested never to agree with England, insomuch that the most part of your friends are slain; but whom can you blame for that but only your own self-will? For if you had agreed to this godly marriage, there needed no Christian blood to be shed.

For Gods sake, remember yourself now in your old age, and seek to have an honourable peace, which cannot be without this marriage. And what a memorial it would be to you for ever, if you could be an instrument for that.

If I should write so long a letter as I could find matter with the wrong of your part and the right of mine, it were too tedious for you to read, but for as much as I purpose, God willing, to come to Carlisle shortly, after Easter, I will keep it in store to tell you myself, for I am sure you will not refuse coming to me, although my uncle George and the laird of Drumlanrig speak against it, who I know would be glad to see you in your grave, although they flatter you to your face.

My uncle George hath said, as divers Scotchmen have told me, that though you had sons, he would be heir and make them all bastards; but my Lord, if God send you no more sons, and I live after you, he shall have little part thereof, or else many a man shall smart for it.

Thus leaving to declare to you father of my mind till I may speak with you myself, I commit you to the keeping of Almighty God, who send you long life with much honour.

By your humble daughter

Margaret Lennox[1]

Despite Margaret's plea to meet him, Angus did not go to Carlisle. Instead he made his falconer, James Lindsay, write to his daughter's falconer, a fellow Scotsman called William Paterson, that he had 'a promising cast of the famous Tantallon hawks for his mews, if his Lord would send him across the Border for them'.

William Paterson, largely unnoticeable in his working-man's clothes, arrived safely at Tantallon. Taken into the kitchen, he regaled the servants and his fellow falconer with all his Yorkshire news. Then, hearing of his arrival, Angus sent him a message to meet him at dawn the next morning in the centre of the castle green.

As the light of the rising sun slanted across the North Sea, they met in the centre of the grass grown court where listeners were safely out of range.

To anyone glancing from a window, they must have seemed a strange pair. The earl, still erect despite his age but with his once red hair and beard now turned grey, a doublet thrown over the steel breastplate to protect him against the wind. Beside him, the falconer in his homespun breeches and linen smock, edging closer to hear his words.

Firstly he asked for news of the family, in particular the little Lord Darnley, a prodigy, so he had been told. Then, dropping his voice to a whisper, he asked, 'Is there no secret thing thou are bidden to show me?'

'Nothing special,' said Paterson, 'but to fetch the hawks,' but then he added significantly that his master, Lord Lennox, while glad to hear he was in good health, hoped that he would be 'more kind to him nor he had been in times past ...'

Paterson must have been previously to Tantallon, for Angus then instructed him to tell Margaret that she 'is the thing in the world I love best, and my Lord her husband, and that young boy there – for my children are dead that thou sawest'.[2]

23

THE GOLDEN BOY

Margaret's anxiety for the welfare of her young son is the more understandable given that his elder brother had died in her absence when only a few months old. Not unnaturally, both she and Matthew adored this boy, who, largely as the result of so much attention, is known to have been precocious from an early age. The fact that his grandfather had heard of it even in Scotland, shows that he was already remarkable both for his height – he was exceptionally tall for his age – and for his scholastic achievements which proved him a clever child. In addition to this, with his fair hair and blue eyes, he was an unusually handsome boy.

Margaret and Matthew did have other children, eventually eight in all, but none that could hold a candle to Henry, at least in their eyes. Henry, moreover, was healthy, something unusual in Tudor times when ailments of all kinds, particularly smallpox and the dreaded sweating sickness, caused devastating mortality particularly amongst the young. At least a third of all children died within their first year.

Matthew, and particularly Margaret, who was much the stronger character of the two, envisaged a spectacular future for this greatly treasured son, who, through his parents, had a claim to the thrones of both Scotland and England. A brilliant marriage was a prospect, perhaps even with the little Queen of Scotland, now, thanks to her French mother's wisdom, safely conveyed to France. The focus of his parents' ambition, Henry seemed to be heading for what, by anyone's standards, had to be a fortunate life.

Not only his parents loved him. From an early age, almost from the moment of his birth, William Taylor, the man specially chosen by his mother, slept in a truckle cot beside his bed. Then, as he reached the age of 4, his mother found him a tutor, this time a cleric, a Scot named John Elder, a native of Caithness, who, having studied in the universities of St Andrews, Aberdeen and Glasgow, had become a canon in the Collegiate Church of Dumbarton. He had followed Matthew to England on the forfeiture, by the Scottish government, of the Lennox estates. However, it was on the recommendation of Matthew's brother, Robert Stuart, the Bishop of Caithness, that Elder was recommended for the all important position of tutor to the young Lord Darnley, Henry's title from birth.[1]

Once in England, having sworn his allegiance to Henry VIII, Elder had won his way into favour by addressing a 'Proposal' for the uniting of Scotland and England through the marriage of Mary Queen of Scots to Henry's son Prince Edward. Decrying the Scottish bishops, and in particular Cardinal Beaton, as agents of the devil or 'Beelzebub's fleshmoners' in his words, he promised the support of the Highlanders, of whom he said he was one.

This 'Proposal' given to Henry on an illustrated parchment scroll, was written in an exceptionally fine hand, although not in the italic script that his pupil, at that age no doubt reluctantly, was forced to learn. Elder also taught Henry Latin, which he began at the age of 5, but it was another tutor, Arthur Lallart, who was hired specifically to teach him French. This language must have come easily to him, his father being bilingual and his mother having learnt to speak it, if not fluently, when as a young girl she allegedly spent some time with her father in France.

The ritual of the Lennox household, as has been described by a contemporary, was no less grand than that of a royal household of the Catholic faith. First thing in the morning the family and their servants attended Mass in the private chapel. Then, as the members of the family retired to their own apartments, the servants began laying out the trestle tables in the Great Chamber. Catholic families dined early, it being necessary to starve before Mass. The earl's table, standing on a carpet beneath a cloth of state, and the knight's table below it, were set with knives and spoons, forks being then a novelty and not in common use. The servants, sitting below the silver salt dish, while given a knife to cut their meat, had otherwise to make do with their fingers. The Yeoman of the Pantry set wine on the sideboard while the Yeoman of the Buttery produced the ale. Then it was the turn of the Carver, to cut slices of bread from each loaf and taste them to make sure they were not poisoned, an ever-present fear. This done, the Carver, together with the Sewer and the Cup-bearer, went downstairs through the Great Hall to the kitchen from where they emerged, bearing huge platters of food. On state occasions they were joined by the chief officers of the household, the Steward, Comptroller and Treasurer, the whole process being so extended that dishes, by the time they reached the Great Chamber, must have been distinctly tepid, if not actually stone cold.

Nonetheless this did not seem to matter, for dinner was a happy occasion with much conversation and laughter amongst the adults and even the Lennox children, who are known to have dined with their parents from quite an early age. Indeed, it was largely for their benefit that Margaret had retired from court, being determined, above all things, to oversee the education and development of Henry, her precious son.

Henry Darnley was nearly 6 when the Queen Dowager of Scotland, Mary of Lorraine, came to London in November 1551. His mother, Margaret, as half-sister to the late King James and aunt to the reigning king, had to be summoned to court; her husband, although equally well connected, had been exiled as a traitor to Scotland and thus was not be presented to her, as neither was his young son.

Margaret, although deeply offended, had no choice but to comply. Her rancour was mollified, however, when Mary of Lorraine received her most warmly at the Bishop of London's palace. There also was her cousin Frances, daughter of the Duchess of Suffolk, from whom she had inherited her beauty. Now the Marchioness of Dorset, Frances came with her daughter, Lady Jane Grey, who in contrast to herself was a shy and serious girl, devoted to the reformed religion. Together they escorted the Scottish queen from the Bishop's palace to the presence of the young Edward VI. Mary of Loraine then insisted that it was Margaret who should sit beside her in the carriage during the stately procession from St Paul's to Westminster and again on the return.

It was while she was in London, or very shortly afterwards, that Margaret received a desperate plea from her father, beseeching her to come and see him while he was still alive. It was no use asking Mary of Lorraine, who at that time was not the Regent of Scotland, for a passport, so instead she applied to the Duke of Northumberland, who had now succeeded the Duke of Somerset as Lord President of the Council. He discussed the matter with his confidential man of business, the lawyer William Cecil.

I pray you, remember what I showed you concerning the Lady Lennox, you and I seeming to be of one mind. Nevertheless as I hear no word mentioned of her husband, who, if he mind to remain here, and also keeping her childer within the realm and circumspectly looked to in her absence, the danger can be nothing. And further, I remember that her husband dare not come within the realm of Scotland, because of a deadly feud between the Governor's [Arran's] blood and him.[2]

Northumberland concluded by expressing his doubts as to why she wanted to go to Scotland at all.

Marry touching her father's inheritance I am sure she can have no profit … except she would refuse her habitation here, and remain there, as I doubt not but all my lords do know it to be likely and true. Wherefore it museth me to think what the occasion should be that moveth her father to seek to have her come so far only to speak with him; but some mystery there must be in it, whatsoever it be, as knoweth the Lord, who have you in his keeping. At Chelsea, this Sunday, the 11th of December, 1552.[3]

The king's council, despite the views of its president, did not grant the visa immediately. Persisting, she tried again in the following spring of 1553. This time, having agreed to all Northumberland's stipulations, she put forward the reason for urgency in that she was again expecting a child and wished to get back from Scotland to her own house, in time for her lying-in.

Northumberland, now much involved in arranging the marriage of his son Guildford to Lady Jane Grey, wrote once more to Cecil telling him to expedite the passport of the Lady Margaret Douglas, as he still termed her, to Scotland by the 8th April, actually the next day.[4]

Margaret reached Tantallon, in all probability travelling in a litter due to her pregnancy, in time to see her father before he died. With her went her priest, Sir John Dicconson, who stayed with him to give him the extreme unction of the Roman Catholic Church, the faith to which she herself so resolutely still adhered.

She may still have been in Scotland when the news came that on 6 July 1553 her nephew, Edward VI, had died of the tuberculosis with which he had struggled so bravely during what was, even in those days, a tragically short span of life.

24

'A MOST VICTORIOUS AND TRIUMPHANT PRINCESSE'

I t soon became plain that Northumberland had a reason for speeding Margaret's visit to Scotland. Knowing that the king was fatally ill, he wanted her out of the way. While Henry was dying, Northumberland had persuaded him to make a 'Devise of the Succession', which excluded his half-sisters and left the Crown to Northumberland's daughter-in-law, Lady Jane Grey, through whom, he believed, he would reign supreme.

At Temple Newsam in Yorkshire, Margaret, while still in her lying-in chamber, waited with great anxiety to hear what had become of Princess Mary. Soon came word that she was at Kenninghall in the south of Norfolk, the house confiscated from the Duke of Norfolk, still held prisoner in the Tower. From there, on 9 July, Mary had written to Queen Jane's council in London demanding that they denounce her as, by her father's will, she herself was the rightful queen. Under Northumberland's dominance, the council promptly, as was expected, repudiated her claim; it was then learned that he was heading to Norfolk with an army to take Mary prisoner and convey her to the Tower.

Nothing, it seemed could save her. Margaret waited in acute anxiety, while Matthew, apparently unwilling to commit himself to what seemed a

hopeless cause, waited to see what would occur. Then, almost unbeliev-
ably, they heard the most wondrous news. Men throughout East Anglia
were rising, surging like an unstoppable tide to support Mary in her bastion
of Kenninghall.

Soon she was known to have moved to Framlingham, the twelfth-century
castle of the Howards given to Mary by her brother shortly before his death.
There, as her colours flew over the gateway of the great curtain wall, men
appeared in their thousands, armed with everything from guns to pitch-
forks, to proclaim her their rightful queen.

Next she was acclaimed at Norwich, from whence came more men and
arms as the leading landowners of Suffolk, including Lord Wentworth, clad
in full armour, rode up to Framlingham to declare Mary their queen. Under
the command of the Earl of Sussex, her army prepared to do battle with
Northumberland, nearly 30 miles away,

But as Northumberland reached Cambridge he was told that in London,
the council, headed by the Earl of Arundel, had decided that Mary, as her
father's daughter, was the rightful heir to the Crown. Arundel himself rode
to Framlingham, where, on 19 July, on bended knee before her, he told her
that she now was queen.

The coronation of Queen Mary, on 1 October 1553, took place at
Westminster Abbey. Surprisingly, her cousin and greatest friend, Margaret
Lennox, was not present, due to the fact that after her return from Scotland
she had given birth to a baby, which, as so often happened in those days of
dreadful infant mortality, very shortly died.

Shortly after the coronation, however, Margaret was certainly at Mary's
court, as the French ambassador de Noailles reported that the Princess
Elizabeth was much annoyed that her sister made their cousins Margaret
Lennox and Frances Dorset take precedence over her, despite the fact that
the latter's daughter (Lady Jane Grey or Dudley as she by then had become)
was closely imprisoned in the Tower. Elizabeth, who had so much of her
father's character, from this time on disliked Margaret, partly on account of
their difference in religion but also because she thought that Margaret influenced her half-sister against her, as she was always too ready to believe.

Fortunately, Margaret was back at Temple Newsam when the Protestant
rebellion, led by Thomas Wyatt, threatened the City of London and the very
life of the queen. Wyatt, always rebellious, had witnessed the horrors of the

Inquisition when his father had taken him to Spain. Hating the Spanish thereafter, on Mary's decision to marry Prince Philip, he had led a party of protestant protestors, purportedly in the name of Princess Elizabeth, from Kent. By the time that the news reached Yorskshire, Margaret would only have heard of how it had ended with Wyatt's supporters deserting him after Mary, with a rousing speech at the Guildhall, rallied the Londoners to her side. The rebels who did reach Tyburn (now Hyde Park Corner) made for the city, but, trapped in the narrow streets, they were decimated by the pikes, swords and cudgels of the armed men of London.

No one rejoiced more greatly than did Margaret on hearing that Mary was safe and the leader of the rebellion against her in the Tower. Nonetheless, perhaps she felt some sympathy for Thomas Wyatt. It had, after all, been none other than his father of the same name, then himself a prisoner, who, when she with her first love Thomas Howard had been sent to the Tower, had been the inspiration of the smuggled verses of poetry which she and her lover had exchanged.

The father had been pardoned, but no mercy was given to the son. Tried on a count of treachery, he offered no defence, but on the scaffold he swore that Elizabeth had not been in any way involved in the rising, which had it been successful would have made her a Protestant queen.

Most tragically, however, Wyatt was not the only one to die. Northumberland, tried and convicted of treachery, had been executed in August 1553. A month after his arrest, his son, Guildford Dudley, together with his wife, the former Lady Jane Grey, to whom Mary, on her accession, had shown mercy, had been sent to imprisonment in the Tower. Mary had hoped to release them, but now as the Duke of Suffolk, Jane's father, was proved to have been involved in the rebellion, her councillors insisted that it was too dangerous for them live. Faced with this ultimatum, Mary, with utmost reluctance, gave the order for their execution, and on 12 February 1554 first Guildford and then Jane were beheaded before the Tower.

Margaret Lennox, thankfully, was with her children at Temple Newsam when her cousin, the quiet little Lady Jane Grey, who had never wanted to be queen, died for the ambition of her father-in-law in which she had been so unwillingly involved.

Meanwhile, at Temple Newsam Henry Darnley, the focus of his mother's affection, was continuing to show exceptional promise at the age of only 8.

It would seem to have been at Margaret's instigation that, under the guid-
ance of his tutor John Elder, the little boy laboriously translated Sir Thomas
More's *Utopia* from the original Latin into English. The result was sent to
Queen Mary, who was so touched by his thoughtfulness and delighted with
his progress that she sent a special messenger galloping up to Yorkshire
with presents which included a rich gold chain. Henry may or may not have
been delighted. Dictated to by his mother, he had to remain indoors to write
a letter of thanks.

The presence of John Elder, leaning over his shoulder, emerges in the
faint lines on the paper between which the little boy wrote, in terms which
must have been dictated to him, so sycophantic is his prose.

Lyke as the Monuments of ancient authors, most triumphaunte, moste victorious, and moste gracious Princesse, declare how that a certane excellent,
Timotheus Musicus, was wounte with his swete proporcioned and melodi-
ous armonye to enflame Alexander the greate Quonquerour and King of
Macedonia to civill warres, with a most fervent desire; evenso, I remembering
with myself oftentimes how that (over and besides suche manifolde benefites
as your Highness heretofore haith bestoued on me) it haith pleased your moste
excellente Majestie laitlie to accepte a little Plote of my simple penning,
which I termed Vtopia Nova; for the which it being base, vile, and maimed,
your Maiestie haithe given me a riche cheane of golde. The noyse (I saye)
of such instrumentes, as I heire now and then, (although ther melody diffre
muche from the swete strokes and sounds of King Alexanders Timotheus)
do not only persuade and move, yea pricke an spurre me forwarde, to ende-
voure my wittes daylie (all vaniities set aparte) to virtuous lerning and study,
being therto thus encouraged, so oftentimes by your Maiseties manifolde
benefites, giftes and rewardes; but also I am enflamed and stirred, even now
my tendre aige not withstanding, to be served by Your Grace , wishing every
haire in my heade for to be a wourthy souldiour, of that same self hert, mynde,
and stomake that I am of. But wher as I perceave that neither my wite, power,
nor yeares ar at this present corresponding unto this, my good will; thes
shall be therefore (most gracious Princesse) most humbly rendring unto your
Maiestie immortall thankes for your riche Cheane, and other your Highnes
syndrie giftes, gyven unto me without anny my deservinges, from tyme to
tyme. Trusting in God, one day, of my moste bounden duetie, to endevour my

self with my faithful hertie service, to remembre the same. And being afraid, with thes my suerflous woordes to interturbe (God forfende) Your Highness, whois moste excellent Maiestie is always and specially now, occupied in most weightie maters, thus I make an end: praing unto Almightie God, most humbly and faithfully to preserve, keipe, and defende your Maiestie, long reigning oeuer us all, your true and faithfull subjectes, a most victorious and triumphant Princesse, Amen.

From Temple Newsome, the xxviii of Marche, 1554.

Your Maiesties moste bounden and obedient

Subjecte and seruaunt,

Henry Darnley.[1]

25

A Conspirator's Smile

Following Thomas Wyatt's execution, Princess Elizabeth had been held in custody. Taken first through the Traitor's Gate to the Tower, she believed, as the arch of the dark stone building closed above her, that she would be the next to die. Despite Wyatt swearing on the scaffold that she was totally innocent of any involvement in his attempt to overthrow her sister and make her queen, she knew that the headsman's axe was ready, sharpened after use for Jane Grey. Daily she waited to be summoned and led as a traitor to her death. But, surprisingly, Mary was merciful, allowing after some time that Elizabeth should be held under house arrest at Woodstock, near Oxford.

In her absence, Margaret Lennox, as the nearest kinswoman to the Crown, was first lady at the wedding of Queen Mary to Prince Philip, son of the Holy Roman Emperor Charles V, who, on the eve of his wedding, created him King of Naples and Duke of Milan.

The marriage took place on 25 July, appropriately the feast of St James, the patron saint of Spain. The ceremony was held in the ancient cathedral of Winchester, thought to be safer than London, where protests against the queen marrying a Roman Catholic foreigner might still have been raised. During the ceremony Margaret Lennox, as mistress of the robes and purse bearer, was in close attendance on the bride. Queen Mary was dressed in regal magnificence in a gown of white satin beneath a mantle of cloth of gold, glittering with precious stones. At one point in the service King Philip, as then was customary when promising to endow a wife with worldly goods, put no less than three handfuls of gold and silver on the Bible. Margaret was pushing it quickly into the queen's purse, when Mary, catching her eye, gave her a conspirator's smile.

One observer of the wedding was Henry Darnley's tutor, John Elder, apparently in charge of his pupil. He described it all in detail to his mentor Robert Stuart, Bishop of Caithness, younger brother of Matthew Lennox. In addition he sent him specimens of Henry Darnley's scholastic progress, some pages of translations from Latin into English, of which Elder was inordinately proud. Explaining to his uncle that the boy was not yet 9, he told him that, for one of his age, he showed amazing ability in speaking and writing both Latin and French, 'and in sundry other virtuous qualities, whom also God and nature hath endowed with a good wit, gentleness and favor'.[1]

This letter, dated from London, on New Year's Day 1555, proves that the Lennox family were at that time still at court. Princess Elizabeth, told of it, apparently decided that far from being the angelic genius of his tutor's estimation, young Henry Darnley was in fact a precocious brat, an opinion which as he got older, she notably failed to change. As for Margaret, his mother, Elizabeth became convinced that it was she who was advising her sister to keep her a prisoner at Woodstock, an accusation Margaret categorically denied. 'Never in my life, I had, or meant to have, any such words with the Queen Mary.' she emphatically declared, but Elizabeth, who once her mind was made up seldom changed it, continued to regard her as enemy on whom she planned revenge.

26

DISPUTED INHERITANCE

Margaret's third son was born at Temple Newsam in 1556. Perhaps in memory of Charles Howard, she called him Charles. His birth was the reason why she could not travel up to Tantallon when word came that her father, now in his sixty-ninth year, was dying. Instead she sent her priest, Sir John Dicconson, in whose arms he died at Tantallon in the fierce cold of the winter month of January 1557.

Dicconson had made the acquaintance of Margaret's father when, following her own visit, she had left him at Tantallon in the spring of 1553. He knew of Angus' resentment over the letter she had written to him after he had refused to let her come to Tantallon when she was almost at the door. Guessing at duplicity, he contrived to lay his hands on the old earl's papers after he had died. Sure enough, amongst them he found confirmation of all that he had feared. In his will Angus had decreed that after the deaths of his two young sons by the Lady Maxwell, there was no entail on his daughter and that he was minded to have the same entailed on the Earl of Morton, one of his nephews.[1]

The nephew, James Earl of Morton, was none other than the Master of Morton, one of the outlawed relations to whom, at her father's request, she had given sanctuary to save them from imprisonment in 1548. As already related, it was Margaret's priest, Dicconson, whom she had left at Tantallon to give the last rights to her dying father, who had taken his will to the Scottish head of Civil Law and had it stopped. Morton, however, insisting that his bequest from Angus was legal, assumed both the lands and titles of his late uncle.

On learning from her priest what had happened, Margaret was understandably furious, and from then on, in defiance of her cousin, continued to sign herself Lennox and Angus.

Not content to let the matter rest, she asked Queen Mary to intercede with Mary of Lorraine (for the last three years, following the resignation of Châtelhérault, Regent of Scotland) to honour her claims as heiress of her father's titles and estates. It was not a good time. War between Scotland and England was about to break out again and the Queen Regent herself was terminally ill.

Nonetheless, from her sickbed she managed to dictate an official application, which was taken in person by the lawyer Doctor Laurence Hussey to the Scottish Chancery. At this point the French ambassador to Scotland, Monsieur d'Oysell, aware of the value of the lands involved, advised the Queen Regent to declare them forfeited to the Crown. On 22 January 1557, writing to his predecessor de Noailles, now back in France as Bishop of Dacqs (or Dax), an ancient city of Gascony on the Loire, he told him what had occurred.

Monsieur

I can add nothing to the dispatch of du Faultrey, but the death of the Earl of Angus [*sic*], of whom Lady Lennox is the principal heiress, and that I much think that the Queen of England will favour as much as she can the claims of that lady to the succession, and that she will do all she can, by one way or another, for that purpose. I pray you to take heed of that, and employ all the pains you can to discover what they mean to do about it where you are.

For my part, I have had the boldness to advise this Queen [Mary of Lorraine] to seize a strong place named Tanrasson [Tantallon] which pertained to the late Earl; and at all events, and for many sound reasons ... I hold that there ought not to be any other hairess to that succession but the young Queen of Scotland ...[2]

Soon after writing this, Monsieur d'Oyseil announced that an English agent was waiting at Berwick for a passport. This proved to be Lady Margaret's agent, Doctor Laurence Hussey, who rode from Edinburgh to Stirling Castle on 5 April 1557 to have an interview with the Queen Regent. Mary of Lorraine was sympathetic to Margaret, fellow Catholic as she was, but, as she pointed out in a letter to Queen Mary in England, 'she stands in some cases far different from the privileges that are common to the subjects of this realm'.

By this she was intimating that Margaret was the wife of a man, who, for his association with Henry VIII, had been outlawed by the Scottish government. Thanks to the influence of Mary of Loraine, Margaret's case was brought before the Chancery but was disallowed on the grounds that her husband, the Earl of Lennox, did not have any civil rights.

However, Margaret did not give up; by permission of the queens of both England and Scotland, on the following 14 November a meeting took place between Lord Wharton, warden of the English marches, and Kirkaldy of Grange, one of the Lords of the Congregation, as the Protestant lords who adhered to the Reformation were called. When Lord Wharton asked whether it would be possible for the Lennoxes to return to Scotland, Kirkaldy prevaricated. But he did agree that they ought to have Tantallon Castle – held since the death of Angus by the Laird of Craigmiller for the Crown – returned to them. This, as he pointed out, would ensure the support of the Douglasses to the Queen Regent, with whom the Lady Margaret was known to be on good terms.

Told of this happening, Morton then made a contract of marriage between his son Archibald, designated Angus' heir, with the daughter of d'Oysell, who had much influence with Mary of Lorraine.

The argument over the Angus inheritance was still undecided when Tom Bishop of all people, the man Matthew most trusted as his secretary, betrayed him to Queen Mary of England as a heretic. Mary, by now extremely ill, for some reason believed Bishop and according to his own word, without telling Margaret, renewed his pension 'and, to the end of her Majesty's days in the affairs of Scotland trusted me where she did not her deare cousing of Levanax'.[3]

This seems hardly credible; yet Bishop was so plausible that Mary, paranoid in her fear of heresy, may, in her last illness, have become distrustful even of Margaret, for so many years her greatest friend.

While determined to win the title which was rightly hers, Margaret also badly needed the income from the Angus estates. Matthew, for his allegiance to the English king, had lost not only his land of the Lennox in Scotland but also, thanks to the alliance between that country and France, all his land in France. Reduced to living on the 5 marks a day which Matthew was allowed for his war service, they were so desperate for money that, according to Bishop, they were selling timber, bark and stone from the estate and even stripping lead from the roof of Jerveaux Abbey.

They were impoverished; however, they still managed to find enough money to send their son's tutor to France to elicit the help of Matthew's younger brother, John Stuart, in presenting their case to the young Queen of Scots, still in France since her escape from Scotland in July 1548. John Stuart, the Sieur d'Aubigny (the title inherited from the great uncle who had brought them up as boys) owed his brother a favour for fighting for the French king: he had been taken prisoner at the Battle of St Quentin in 1557 and released only thanks to Matthew paying part of his ransom. John Elder went out to France, armed with some of the examples of his pupil's penmanship, which he proudly presented to the young queen, now 16 years old. Promised as she was to the dauphin, she nonetheless showed interest in Darnley, as the prodigy which his tutor claimed him to be. Also intrigued were the French princes and the King of Navarre.

Elder came home with a much welcome present of 50 crowns from the Cardinal of Lorraine to the Lennoxes, as was discovered by Bishop, the indefatigable spy. Bishop also sent word to London that Matthew Lennox was a victim of what appears to have been a virulent form of influenza, which was sweeping the country at the time. To help him recover, the family moved to Settringham House in the south-east of Yorkshire, which, as Bishop hastened to report, was not only a healthful location but conveniently near to Bridlington, a port much used by vessels from the Continent traversing the North Sea.

Following Elder's visit, the Sieur d'Aubigny came over to Scotland to be given a post in the household of Mary of Lorraine. Involved in raiding across the Border, he was unlucky enough to be captured for the second time. Held captive in an English prison, he once more asked his brother for money to pay a ransom to set him free. Matthew sent a Scotsman named Halbert with bank bills as requested, but he then tried to get some recompense by sending word to Queen Mary that his brother could tell her much of what was going on in Scotland at the court of Mary of Lorraine. Margaret then sent

Arthur Lallard, one of her son's tutors, to her brother-in-law, but by the time he reached the prison, d'Aubigny had somehow escaped, no doubt by bribing his jailers with his brother's money, and returned to France. Lallard retrieved his possessions, which included a Roman Catholic prayer book which had belonged to Matthew when he was a young man in France.

Queen Mary, told of this, despatched the Bishop of Durham to Matthew's bedside for the good of his soul. It proved to be one of her last actions before she herself died on 17 November 1558.

Margaret was chief mourner, heading Mary's other ladies-in-waiting as the chariot bearing the queen's coffin, with her wooden painted effigy lying on top, to Westminster Abbey to be buried in a vault in the chapel of Henry VII. As the coffin was lowered, Margaret was the first of her household offices to break her white staff of office and throw it into the grave. She had lost the cousin who, despite their recent difference, had once been her greatest friend.

27

FROM ENGLAND'S COURT TO FRANCE

The Lennoxes, on Elizabeth's succession, hastened at once to her court where, as she wrote to William Cecil, they were 'most graciously received'.

Queen Elizabeth went so far as to enquire after Matthew's health, and having listened to the symptoms of his illness, she advised Margaret never to leave his side. Whether this was a way of getting rid of her is debateable. On parting she apparently assured her that if in any trouble she should apply directly to William Cecil who, if at all possible, would comply with all she asked.

William Cecil, son of minor Welsh nobleman, who, after proving himself a clever lawyer to both Henry VIII and Edward VI, was now, as Queen Elizabeth's secretary, the most powerful man in the land. Amongst Cecil's confederates was George Earl of Morton, described as 'the brother of his soul'. It would appear that shortly after the Queen Elizabeth's accession, Cecil used his influence in the Star Chamber of Inquisition in Westminster Palace to cross-question one of the Lennox's servants. Presumably the man was apprehended while the Lennoxes were in London for some reason unknown. Probably under torture, the man or woman revealed how

Margaret's priest Dicconson had taken her father's letter, deposing his estates and titles to his nephew, to the Justice Clerk Bellenden in Edinburgh and thereby had succeeded in getting his will revoked.

Ignoring the underhand dealings of Lord Morton, or the more legal claims of the grandson and heir of Sir George Douglas (her hated uncle) named by her father as his heir, Margaret continued to add the title of Angus to her name. She was bold in her assertion that this title, at least, was her birthright. Her defiance was fired by hatred of the English Parliament, which, in the name of the people of England, had declared King Henry's younger daughter to be their rightful queen.

Margaret had lived with the hope that, because of their shared religion, Mary would name her as her successor rather than the Protestant half-sister with whom she had long disagreed. While waiting on Elizabeth in London, subservient to her every wish, she inwardly raged at the knowledge that had only justice been done, their positions would have been reversed. The red-haired, straight-backed young woman at whose feet she had been forced to kneel, for no reason other than that of the new established creed, had robbed her of her right to the English throne.

Returning sadly to Yorkshire, Margaret did have one consolation in that despite her insistence of the English prayer book being used in churches throughout the land, the Mass could be celebrated in private, as happened at Settrington House. On the evidence of the spies within her household (perhaps the one who had told of the revoking of her father's will) she is known to have had the curtains of her own bed, as well as those of her son, hung with holy relics, to which she showed great reverence. Likewise she told the beads of her rosary, and with the enforced attendance of both her son and her husband, celebrated Mass every day.

The Lennoxes are known to have been at Settrington when they heard that the French King Henri II, jousting with the Count de Montgomery, Captain of the Garde Ecossaise, had been killed. This meant that Mary Queen of Scots, married as she was to Francois, the former dauphin and now the king, was the Queen of France.

Immediately it was decided that, whatever the risks involved, Henry Darnley would go to France to congratulate Francois and Mary on their accession. The journey had to be made in secret. To apply to Queen Elizabeth for a passport would be a waste of time. Therefore, heavily cloaked, and probably calling themselves merchants, Henry and his tutor, John Elder, set off from Bridlington in a trading ship in which they safely made the crossing to Dieppe.

Arriving at the court at Chambord, they were greatly assisted by Henry's uncle, John Stuart d'Aubigny. An exceptionally handsome and charming man, d'Aubigny had now succeeded the unfortunate Compte de Montgomery, a splinter from whose lance had entered the French king's eye, as Captain of the Garde Écossaise. It was d'Aubigny who arranged a secret meeting between Henry and his cousin, Mary Queen of Scots, and her husband, the 15-year-old King of France. Both were in mourning for the late king, Mary wearing the *deuil blanc*, the white mourning of a diaphanous white veil falling from a white hood, which, with strands of her auburn hair showing beneath it, suited her so well.

The first meeting of Henry and Mary was uneventful. Little could either of them guess what lay in store. Mary was charmed by the polished manners of the tall, fair-haired boy who bowed before her as he presented a letter from his father, requesting the restoration of his Scottish estates. This, without evidence to prove the authenticity of what he asked, she had to refuse, but forthwith invited both her visitors to her husband's coronation and gave Henry a present of a 1,000 crowns.

At the coronation, which took place at Rheims on 18 September 1559, Mary Queen of Scots, as a reigning sovereign, was not crowned as a consort. Casting off her mourning for one day, she appeared beautifully dressed, her hair a shining halo, even brighter than her many jewels. The eyes of Sir Nicholas Throckmorton, Queen Elizabeth's ambassador in France, like those of most of the congregation, were quickly drawn to her. But also, in the throng, he recognised the austere figure of John Elder, whom he had met before.

He did not realise the identity of the tall young man who stood beside Elder, but he did report 'how a young gentleman, an Englishman or a Scottishman, who had no beard, was received with great distinction by the King and Queen of France and Scotland, Francis II, and Mary Stuart, at Chambord, where they were keeping their Christmas festival. The interviews of the young stranger were long and private, both with the King and with the Duke de Guise.'[1]

Throckmorton, for some unknown reason, then seized the chance to make trouble between Queen Elizabeth and Margaret Lennox. John Elder, he claimed, had taken details of the persecutions of the Protestants by Bonner, Bishop of London, in Queen Mary's time. Naming Cardinal Pole, Lady Salisbury's son, as the source of this information, he claimed him to be 'as dangerous for the matters of England as any I know; wherefore it were done that good regard were had to such as he is acquainted with in England.' – a clear indication of the Lennoxes.

Great was the rejoicing at Settrington when Henry and his tutor returned from France unscathed. Matthew Lennox, still largely an invalid, was disappointed to hear that his plea for the return of his estates in Scotland was rejected. Nonetheless he was at that time receiving overtures, both from Mary of Lorraine and her opponents, the members of the Congregation, to whom Arran (the Duc de Châtelhérault) was now allied.

28

'THE GREAT REVENGE THAT YE MIGHT HAVE OF YOUR ENEMIES'

In the summer of 1559, Matthew was roused from his lethargy by a visit from a Captain Borthwick, a one-time companion-in-arms on the Borders when fighting for the English cause. His old companion-in-arms arrived with the suggestion that Matthew might find it expedient to come to the aid of the ill and harassed Queen Regent, at whose behest he had come. Margaret, overhearing the conversation, sternly forbade him to have anything to do with a man whom she suspected to be an enemy agent. Borthwick, furious at her interference, was only slightly mollified by being introduced to Henry Darnley, whom he found both charming and courteous.

Borthwick rode on to London, where, in secret, he met the French ambassador, the Comte de Noailles. Complaining bitterly to him that Lennox was ruled by his wife, he extolled the virtues of young Henry, calling him 'the nearest person in the royal succession to both realms, by right of his father in Scotland, if Mary Stuart, Queen of France and Scotland has no issue; likewise he is next heir to the throne of England through his mother, Margaret, Countess of Lennox.' De Noailles, however, despite these glowing affirmations of the suitability of the Lennoxes' son to be ruler of both British kingdoms, thoroughly distrusted Borthwick, knowing him, as did Margaret Lennox, to be a most ardent advocate of the reformed religion.

Hardly had Borthwick departed before Matthew received a more definite plea that he should return to Scotland from James Stewart of Cardonald, one of his own former vassals in the Lennox, who lived close to Darnley Castle between Glasgow and Paisley.

> James Stewart of Cardonald to the Earl of Lennox.
>
> My Lord
>
> After my most hearty commendams of servaunce, plesit your Lordship to be remembered the last time that your Lordship's servant, Master Naskit [Nisbit] was in the country, I advertised your Lordship and my Lady's Grace your best remedy that I could find touching your Lordship's affairs in this country, of the which I had no response again, which made belief, as it show indeed, that your Lordship would not proceed no farther at that time; and now the occasion presents that your Lordship may with great honour come to your own.
>
> The great revenge that ye might have of your enemies, which time presently if your Lordship contents not ye sall never come to it again, considering the great occasion it offers of itself. And if your Lordship think it expedient to have the matter dressed, let me knawe your mind either by write or by some special servant whom your Lordship gives credence to, and I trust in God to bring the matter to sic past that your Lordship sall be contented therewith. Referring the rest to your wisdom and discretion, for, as to my part, as sall be evermore ready to do your Lordship the best service I can that your Lordship can require of me. This, after my most humble commendations to my Lady Grace, my Lord Darnely, I pray God have your Lordship and them both in his keeping.[1]

It remains uncertain as to which side the Laird of Cardonald was representing. Mary of Lorraine, as reported by de Noailles to Matthew's servant and French agent, Laurence Nisbet, was offering favourable terms. But Sir Walter Scott believed it to have been a feeler from the Congregation Lords.

Matthew and Margaret, suspicious of both parties, refusing to commit themselves, instead played a waiting game. Nesbit is claimed to have approached de Noailles, the one person they believed they could trust, who advised him to write to Francis and Mary asking for the return of their

Scottish estates. The veracity of this seems uncertain as Nisbet reputedly offered their sons, Henry and the little Charles, as hostages, an arrangement which, in the light of their known adoration, particularly of their eldest son, seems unlikely in the extreme.

Whatever the truth of these proceedings, the knowledge that the Lennoxes, through Nisbet, were claiming their eldest son to be heir presumptive to the throne of England, somehow reached Queen Elizabeth, presumably through her secretary William Cecil. Matthew was on the point of writing to Cecil, asking him to put forward his request to the Queen for a passport for himself and her cousin, his wife, to go to Scotland. Once there, he assured Cecil, 'no one could or would do her Majesty better service than they.'

In confirmation of their intentions, Matthew enclosed a letter from Mary of Lorraine, the Queen Regent, then besieged in Edinburgh Castle by the Lords of the Congregation, enforced by an English army. Desperate for assistance, she tried to bribe them to return to Scotland. To Matthew she offered the rank and estates of Châtelhérault, now denounced as a rebel, and to Margaret the lands and titles of her late father Angus.[2]

On presenting Matthew's letter containing the enclosure to Cecil, Laurence Nisbet was promptly put into the Tower.

On word of this reaching Settrington, Matthew immediately wrote again to Cecil, apologising for his servant and exonerating himself from any complicity in Nisbet's dealing with de Noailles. Nisbet, although interrogated, did not reveal anything of importance. Eventually released, he was certainly with Matthew on a night that neither would forget.

29

OF SOOTHSAYERS
AND SPIES

Margaret got news of the court from a friend, who, careful not to put anything in writing, sent messages through Hugh Allan, a servant who went to and fro London on business connected with the family. At the same time Queen Elizabeth was kept informed of the goings on at Settrington by a man called Forbes, who, while in some way employed in her household, was also a spy for Robert Dudley, the Queen's current favourite, rumoured to be her lover.

Forbes told Dudley that Margaret kept a fool in her house who railed against both Elizabeth and himself. Then he reported Margaret as saying that 'either Queen Mary or the Queen's Majesty Elizabeth behoved to be a bastard' and that all the world knew that Queen Mary had been legitimate. Later, when told that Dudley's wife had been found dead at the bottom of the stairs, Margaret had retorted, 'It was perfectly obvious that he had murdered her.'

In the midst of all this gossip going back and forth from Yorkshire to London, came Margaret's extraordinary prediction that Elizabeth would have a very short life. It turned out that this was misconstrued by Arthur Lallart, one of Henry's tutors, who had tried to fathom the mysteries of the book of prognostications by Nostradamus, first published in Lyons in 1555. Lallart's translation was in fact entirely wrong. The destruction forecast was of 'Powlis steeple' the steeple of St Pauls Cathedral in London, which was mysteriously consumed by fire. Years later an aged mason was to confess, on his deathbed, that he had left a pan of coals burning when he went home from his work. But in the meantime, on the same day, no less than six of Robert Dudley's men, together with some of the Queen's Guard, were killed in St James's Park by what must have been a stroke of lightning.

To help pay the household expenses, Margaret was now boarding young ladies. Thanks to Henry's closing of the nunneries, there was nowhere for young women of aristocratic families in need of accommodation to go other than to private houses. This arrangement was made through the auspices of Francis Yaxley, secretary of Robert Dudley. Yaxley had sent Henry Darnley a turquoise as a gift of friendship, but nonetheless was at loggerheads with Forbes, who continued to report all that went on at Settrington to Queen Elizabeth.

One item of news that he reported was that Lord Gaston, a friend of the Lennoxes, had arrived from France to tell them that King Francois was on the verge of death. Francois in fact died at Orleans in December 1560. Forbes then hastily passed on the word that young Darnley himself had gone there to convey his parent's letters of condolence.

What was Margaret's reaction to the news of Francois' death? Is it fair to imagine that the news made her breath catch in her throat? Certain it is that not long afterwards the idea formulated in her mind that the achievement of her most passionate wish had changed from a dream to reality. Henry, now approaching manhood, handsome as an Adonis, with the royal blood of Stuart and Tudor in his veins, was, as she had known from the moment of his birth, worthy to become a king.

It has even been suggested that, either then or shortly afterwards, the marriage of Mary Stuart to Henry Darnley was arranged between herself and his mother.[1] This assertion cannot be verified, but Henry, on this occasion, certainly left a good impression, of which his uncle d'Aubigny continued to remind the widowed queen.

Queen Elizabeth, when this was related to her, apparently flew into one of the rages for which she was famously renowned. Her temper was not improved when she heard from Forbes that he himself had gone to Scotland, with Lord Gaston, 'about Whitsunday last [1561] and he told me all should be well for my Lord Darnley with the queen'. To this he added that Lord Seton had told him to tell Lady Lennox that 'he would not only spend his living in setting forth my Lord Darnley, but also would spend his blood'.[2]

Besieged by an English army, Mary of Lorraine, the Queen Regent, died in Edinburgh Castle on 11 June 1560. Shortly afterwards a deputation of Lords of the Congregation, consisting of the Earls of Morton and Glencairn and Maitland of Lethington, rode from Scotland to London to thank Queen Elizabeth for her support to their cause. James Douglas, son of Angus' brother, George Douglas, and therefore Margaret's first cousin, had achieved the Morton earldom through marriage. While in England he thought it expedient to make a visit to Margaret in Yorkshire.

This was not the first time that James Douglas, now through his marriage to the insane Elizabeth Douglas, daughter and heiress of the Earl of Morton, had come to stay with the Lennoxes. Born c.1516, he had been in his early thirties when taken prisoner by the English army while besieging his Palace of Dalkeith in 1548. 'Sore hurt on the thigh', taken as a hostage to England, he had been freed together with some of his relations at the intercession of his uncle the Earl of Angus on the condition that they remained under house arrest in one of his daughter's houses, which in this case seems to have been Wressil Castle.

It may have been through conversation with James, at that time styled Master of Morton, that Margaret had first become aware of her father's intention to bypass her own rights to inheritance by making him his heir. His reasons for this seemingly gross infringement of his daughter's constitutional rights, can only be put down to her husband's attack and sacking of the Douglas stronghold of Drumlanrig Castle in the name of the English King Henry. Construing this as treachery, Angus had determined that his land and titles in Scotland should remain with the Douglas family in the person of James Douglas, son of his brother George.

Margaret Lennox, however, since the death of his two infant sons, had remained her father's heiress. Plainly it was to obtain her permission to relinquish her inheritance that her cousin James Morton came to see her, choosing a propitious moment when aware that her husband, Matthew Lennox, was not at home.

James was now a middle-aged man of 44. His portrait shows him a true Douglas, thin faced, with the red hair and beard so typical of his kin. A high stove-pipe hat crowns his head and he wears a doublet topped by a ruff, so fashionable at the time.

He must have been very persuasive, or it may have been due to filial obedience to the father, who despite his recent cruelty had been the idol of her early years, that Margaret agreed to allow her rightful inheritance to pass to him.

Matthew, however, was furious. Returning to discover what had happened, he realised at once that his wife had been deceived. Raging with anger against Morton, her father and the Douglasses as a whole, Matthew declared the agreement to be totally null and void.

30

ARREST

Shortly after Morton's visit, Allan Lallart reported that Mary Queen of Scots had taken ship from France. Margaret waited, torn with anxiety in the knowledge that English warships, known to be off the coast, would certainly intercept the vessel and probably take her prisoner. But no such catastrophe occurred. The next she heard was that the ship had landed safely at Leith. Forbes, within earshot when this happened, saw Margaret sit down and raise her hands to heaven, exclaiming 'How God preserves that Princess at all times.'

Reported to Elizabeth, this gave even further reason for offence. Alan Lallart, however, was despatched at once to Scotland, purportedly to meet the Comte d'Aubigny, who in fact had stayed behind in France. But Alan recognised Lord Gorland, Matthew's youngest brother, who he asked to introduce him to the queen.

Accordingly, just as Mary was about to mount her horse to ride from Stirling to Perth, Lallart pushed his way through her attendants. Then, kneeling before the slim young queen standing tall above him, he paid the Lennoxes' respects, before making the request that their Scottish estates might be returned to them.

The queen, according to Lallart, stated 'That she was but newly returned to her realm, therefore she could not give me such an answer as she would; but all she might do for my lord and my lady, her aunt, she would do at proper time and place, desiring my lady to be always her good aunt, as indeed she knew her to be, with remembrance to them both.'[1]

William Forbes, the spy at Settringham, believing himself discovered, convinced that Margaret was now plotting against him, wrote to Lord Gray, commander of the English army in Scotland, 'that she wrote to Queen Mary against myself'. Then, in another letter to Cecil, which he doubtless showed to Queen Elizabeth, he poured out the most venomous accusations against the woman who had employed him, trusting him implicitly so it seems.

> She frequenteth, by messengers, witches and hath one in her house, that for this two years has told her that she shall be in great trouble, and yet do well enough, for she hopeth for a day the which I trust she shall never see, her doings being espied betimes. She loveth neither God nor the Queen's Majesty, nor yet your honour.[2]

In addition to this extraordinary diatribe, Forbes solemnly declared that he had heard Margaret say that Lord Robert Dudley had killed his wife.

This, it would seem, proved the last straw for Queen Elizabeth, who passionate in her defence of Robert Dudley, would never allow even a whiff of scandal to be attributed to his name. On the excuse that Margaret could be called a traitor for daring to correspond with the queen of a country with which England was officially a war, she ordered the arrest and detention of all of the Lennox family, together with their household staff.

The blow came at Christmas 1561. The family were gathered at Settrington, as doubtless Cecil had guessed, when, with a clattering of hoofs and blowing of trumpets, Queen Elizabeth's messengers arrived with a summons to travel to London immediately. Children, priests, tutors, servants, even the girls sent to board, all had to attend. No excuses were viable. Neither was any delay.

The weather was so cold that the coaches could only move slowly, jolting over frozen ruts in the road. Inside, the passengers, huddled together, moaned over their plight. Margaret in particular lamented, knowing what it would cost. She was all too aware that on arrival, she would have to pay for whatever accommodation could be found. The sweating sickness was then rampant, influenza another risk, and it is thought that two of her little daughters succumbed on that journey although nothing records their deaths.

As they travelled Margaret made plans and told her eldest son Henry exactly what he must do. Arriving in London, some of the entourage were deposited in the prison of the Gate House in Westminster while the Lennox family were housed in Margaret's own suite of chambers in Westminster Palace. In the short winter's day, it was dark by the time the travellers, tired and stiff, climbed out of the carriages which had carried them so far. Then suddenly there was an outcry from the people receiving them. Where was Lord Darnley? He was not with them? Where on earth had he gone?

Margaret pretended astonishment. She thought he had been behind in one of the other coaches. She had no idea where he was. Only one thing emerged for certain. Henry, Lord Darnley, over 6ft tall and hardly missable, had, nonetheless, disappeared.

31

'A VERY WISE AND
DISCREET MATRON'

Henry Darnley was next heard of in France. How he got there remains a mystery. Most probably in disguise, hidden below decks, having made most of the journey by boat.

There is no doubt that Queen Elizabeth and Cecil, once they heard of Henry's being in France, realised that somehow his mother had devised a plan for his going there to court the now widowed Queen of Scots. Unable to punish him personally, their wrath fell on his parents. Margaret was ordered to stay in her rooms in Westminster while Matthew, handed over to the Master of the Rolls, was placed under close arrest in the Tower.

Margaret, her son Charles and, it is thought, her surviving daughter, were then once more held as house prisoners by Sir Richard and Lady Sackville, the queen's great aunt and uncle, in the Charterhouse at Sheen. From there, Margaret, frantically worried about her husband, reportedly utterly despondent in the Tower, wrote repeatedly to Cecil. In one letter, headed 'Sheen, May 14, 1552', she begged him:

Good Master Sekretory

After my right hearty commendations, this is to require of you some comfort concerning my husband's liberty, either to be clearly out of the Tower, which should be most to my comfort, or else at the least some more liberty within it. I have staid in troubling you, for that my hope was to have had some good news. For that I myself do know the Queen's Majesty to be of so gracious, so good, and gentle nature, that if her Highness had been moved for my Lord and me, she would have had some pity of us ere now, considering the long time of trouble we have had, which has been since Christmas. Wherefore I shall beseech you to move her Majesty in this my humble and lowly petition, and that my lord may come to his answer again, for that ye sent me word by Fowler that he stood to the denial of all things laid to his charge. I trust he will not contend or deny any thing of truth, and in so doing my hope is her Majesty will be his good and gracious lady, who never meant to willingly to deserve the contrary. As knoweth God who has you in his keeping.[1]

Fowler, Margaret's messenger, returned a week later with Cecil's answer, which was so unsatisfactory that she wrote to him again on 21 May, demanding to know on what charges they were held.

I have received your answer by my man Fowler, but nothing touching the petitions in my letter, for that ye say there is new matter both against my lord and me, which, when it shall please the Queen's Majesty, I shall be glad to understand, not doubting, with God's grace, but both my lord and I shall be able to acquit ourselves, if right may take place – that our accusers may be brought before us. I assure you I am weary of this life, and would fain receive some comfort from her Majesty; for, as methink, we have had enough punishment for a great offence ... wherefore I shall desire you to be my friend in being a means to the Queen's Majesty, of yourself, for my lord and me, for I think her Highness will give better ear to you than to my letter ... Not withstanding, as her Highness pleasure is I am content; but I shall pray to Him, who is the champion and defender of the innocent to inspire her Majesty's heart toward me according to the good nature I know her Majesty to be of. Declaring this unto her shall bind my lord and me to be yours assuredly.[2]

This appeal did at least force the members of the Star Chamber into action. Cecil was told by Queen Elizabeth to examine Lady Lennox on the allegations of the spy in her household, William Forbes. The notes that he wrote confirm the questions asked of her, which include the sayings of her fool, the other servants and most notably the letters which she and her husband had written to Mary Queen of Scots. What transactions, they demanded to know, had taken place between them and Lord Seton to further their son's suggested marriage to the queen?

She was also asked about her supposed connections with Nostradamus relating to the gift of second sight. When St Paul's steeple was burnt how many men had been killed in St James's Park? More significantly, she was asked to explain her assertion that 'touching the right of the Crown, she would give place to none of the rest'. Cecil himself told her that the Star Chamber was investigating the legality of her claim to the throne of England through her mother. Once again, the old assertion of her parent's supposedly illegal marriage was being dragged up by an Alexander Pringle, who, not surprisingly, turned out to be an agent of the man hanging like an evil genii over the family, Margaret's nephew, James, Earl of Morton.

Knowing that the Berwick herald, Harry Ray, although now an old man, could testify to her mother's statement on her deathbed that she had been legally married to Angus at the time of their daughter's birth, Margaret wrote again to Cecil, insisting that: 'Even as God has made me, so I am, lawful daughter to the Queen of Scots and the Earl of Angus, which none alive is able to make me otherwise. Without doing wrong.'[3]

On the 12 July Margaret did receive an answer from Cecil to the effect that 'the Queen would not grant the Earl of Lennox more liberty in the Tower while he used himself as he did', in other words until he showed more humility to his jailers.[4]

At this point, Margaret was herself very ill with what appears to have been influenza, which gave her 'terrible pains in her head'. However, she was much more worried about her husband than about herself. Told of Matthew's worsening condition in the Tower, she now became convinced that, like her former lover Thomas Howard, he would die. Desperate, she made another appeal, this time to Queen Elizabeth herself, begging her to allow Matthew to share her own imprisonment at Sheen or, if this was not possible, to allow him at least to have what she called 'the liberty of the Tower', to walk about the building and perhaps even stretch his legs on Tower Green.

Needless to say, it met with no response. 'My lord's sickness,' she told Cecil, 'comes only by close keeping and lack of comfort; so that, if it might please her Majesty to suffer him to come to Sheen and to be here as I am, we should think ourselves much bound to her Highness, for otherwise I know he can not continue without danger to of life.'[5]

On 22 July she tried again, asking Cecil to beseech Queen Elizabeth to have consideration of herself, her poor kinswoman, '… and of my husband, who is in close prison without comfort to his nature, and as her Highness knows, not very healthful, having a disease which solitariness is most against, as heretofore, to my comfort, her Majesty hath willed me to cause him always to be in company.'[6]

This last appeal, which seems to have reminded Queen Elizabeth that she herself had once told Margaret that Matthew should never be left alone, did at least draw out an answer as to why she had committed them to prison. It was her conviction, as by now they must have guessed, that they were aiming at a marriage between their son Henry and Mary Queen of Scots.

Fortunately, Henry's tutor, Arthur Lallard, had sworn under oath that his only reason for going to Scotland to see Queen Mary and Matthew's young brother, Monsieur d'Aubigny, had been to ask for the return of Lennoxes' property sequestered by the Scottish Government.

On 24 July, Margaret wrote to Cecil, telling him that while she could not answer for her husband unless she was permitted to see him that 'for my part, except it was for the schoolmaster's going into Scotland without the Queen Majesty's leave, I can remember no offence'.[7]

This produced a sharp retort from Queen Elizabeth: 'That the submission of Lord Lennox must, and not by his wife's teaching.'[8]

Cecil then advised Margaret to appeal to other members of the council, which she did most reluctantly. She was 'not accustomed to write to a Council', so she said. Nonetheless she did write to both the Lord Keeper, Sir Nicholas Bacon, and to Lord Pembroke.[9]

By now, to add to her worries, Margaret was extremely short of money, and on the same day she wrote again to Cecil telling him how she was placed.

Good Master Secretary

I can not cease but trouble you still, till I may receive some comfort, praying you to remember my intolerable griefe, which ariseth divers ways, as well as by my lord's imprisonment, and mine, being thereby separated, as also by impoverishment, which daily increaseth to our utter undoing: as first being in great debt before the beginning of this trouble, and then coming up upon the sudden, having naught but upon borrowing to sustain my charges leaving all goods, though small they be, as well as cattle and household stuff and grounds, without order which now goeth to ruin and decay for lack of looking to, having not any trusty servant [to] spare to redress the same, certain being in prison, and the rest few enow to attend our business here besides. Then the great charges we are at in these parts – one way with my lord and his servant's imprisonment, another way with mine own and children's, and those attending on me and them.

That having naught but upon borrowing to suffice the ordinary charge since my coming up [to London] which shift I have so long made that now it faileth. An' for the small portion of living my lord and I have, the revenue thereof is far unable to suffice the half of the ordinary charges we now be at, beside that we were before hand of divers of our bailiffs, as occasion enforced us into. All of which considered, making my moan to you, my trust is that ye will be a mean to shorten the time of my lord's trouble and mine, beseeching ye, so soon as ye may, to participate the promises of the Queen's Majesty, having confidence that her Highnesses good nature is such that she will not see me utterly impoverished now in my old age, being her Majesty's poor kinswoman ... From Sheen this Saturday.

Your assured friend to my power,

Margaret Lennox and Anguse.[10]

Margaret's pleas remained unanswered, but in October 1562, Queen Elizabeth succumbed to smallpox of which she very nearly died. For weeks, as her life remained in danger, speculation raged as to whom would succeed her in the then imminent expectation of her death. Would it be the Queen of Scotland, or one of the queen's first cousins, namely the Lady Katherine Grey or the Countess of Lennox? In fact it would be none of them. Surprisingly, Elizabeth survived. On 25 October Margaret, yet again writing to Cecil, said, however insincerely, 'Thanks be to God of the Queen's amendment, which is no small comfort to me.'[11]

She wrote again on 12 November asking him to renew her supplication to the queen that Matthew might be released from the Tower. The queen knew how ill her husband was and how bad it was for him to remain in the Tower, so cold and damp at this time of the year; if only he could be transferred to Sheen to be with herself and their children, she would be quite content.

Elizabeth, made more compassionate it would seem by her own near brush with death, finally relented. Matthew was released from the Tower on 26 November and allowed to join Margaret under house arrest at Sheen.

Finally, in February 1563, they were informed by members of the queen's council that 'she had forgiven and forgotten their offence, yet she would not see them'. Freed at last from imprisonment, they were allowed to go home.

32

IN POVERTY
AND SPLENDOUR

The Lennoxes returned to find Settrington nearly ruined. On their hasty departure at the queen's summons, no one had been left properly in charge. Local people, thinking it deserted, had broken into the house and stolen some of the contents. Farm rents had not been collected, cattle had been stolen and buildings left unrepaired.

Margaret, forced to pay for the accommodation of her family and their servants during the whole of their imprisonment, was so impoverished that she actually had to borrow money from the Sackvilles. Nonetheless, once back at Settrington, with typical determination, she began to put things to rights. Then, to her great joy, during the summer, Henry, her beloved elder boy, returned from France.

So happy was she to see him that somehow she found the money to commission the full-length portrait, attributed to Hans Eworth, which now hangs in the Royal Collection. Henry, aged 17, had reached his full height, estimated as being between 6ft 1in and 6ft 4in. He was certainly a head above most men of the time, supposedly the reason why he first attracted the young Queen of Scots, who herself, at 6ft, was accustomed to looking down on most men whom she met. In the portrait, his fair hair and blue eyes are set off by a black doublet, relieved by a white ruff; the legs of an athlete are emphasised by black hose.

Henry stands with his long-fingered hand on the shoulder of his little brother Charles, who, aged 7, is still in skirts, with a crucifix hanging round his neck. The difference in age between them is emphasised by Henry's unusual height, of which his mother was so proud.

In 1564, at Whitsuntide, Matthew Lennox at last was granted permission to return to Scotland. He went with the determination to reclaim his ancestral estates, forfeited by the Scottish government for his adherence to Henry VIII. Margaret, dominant as usual, told him to seek the help of her relations, the Melvilles, Sir James and his brother Robert, then rising powers in Scotland.

Left behind at Settrington, she continued the struggle with the debts and difficulties of trying to restore their lands in Yorkshire so ruined by their enforced absence in London.

The Earl of Westmorland, who apparently she held in her thrall, helped in this enormous task. It was not a romantic liaison. Not even the ever-watchful Forbes, determined to ruin her reputation, could cast a slur on her name as far as this friendship was concerned. Charles, 6th Earl of Westmorland, was a young man of only 20, barely older than Henry Darnley, while Margaret herself would be 50 in the following year.

The link between them was religion. Westmorland, an ardent Catholic, was diametrically opposed to Elizabeth's rule. Already planning rebellion, he turned for assistance to Margaret; in return, in her husband's absence, he helped her to try to resuscitate their run down estates.

It may have been at Westmoreland's suggestion that she tried to sell off some land, estimated to be worth £100. To do this she had to have the queen's permission, the area in question being part of the royal grant, and she carried on a long communication with Cecil, through the auspices of his secretary Francis Yaxley.

33

A DIARIST AT COURT

Matthew reached Edinburgh on 23 September. An anonymous Scottish diarist, who witnessed his arrival, was much impressed by the display of splendour. 'Riding before [him] twelve gentlemen clothed in velvet coats, with chains about their necks, upon fair horses, and behind him thirty other gentlemen and servants riding upon good horses, clothed all in grey livery coats.' Reaching Holyrood, he was received by the queen 'in presence of the most part of the nobility of the realm'.[1]

Acting on his wife's instructions, Matthew immediately contacted her relations, Sir James Melville and his brother Robert (later Lord Melville), who came from Halhill in Fife.

It is now that the man whose first-hand account throws such vivid insight into the happenings of those times, first appears on the scene. Sir James Melville, as he was to become, began writing his diary when he was only 14. It so happened that the Bishop of Valence, who had been on a diplomatic mission to Scotland, had been returning to France when Mary of Loraine had asked him to take James with him to be page of honour to her daughter Mary Queen of Scots. After a horrendous voyage, which involved sailing to Ireland and back before eventually reaching France, James had become a page with the young queen. Later, in the service of the Duke of Montmorency, the constable of France, he had fought for the king, Henri II, against the armies of the King of Spain and the Austrian Holy Roman Emperor. During the battle of St Quentin, in which the French were badly defeated, James was hit on the head with a mace. Pushed by his servant onto a horse, he somehow rode through the enemy lines until he reached a place called La Fer, where an old friend, an Englishman, Mr Harry Killigrew,* held his horse while he sat down in a barber's shop to be treated for the hurt in his head.

Employed thereafter by the Elector Palatine, learning to speak fluent German, he had been sent on a diplomatic mission to France. But while there he had received a summons from Queen Mary's half-brother, the Earl of Moray, and her secretary, William Maitland of Lethington, to return to Scotland on business, which he understood to concern the queen's marriage. Much to the annoyance of the constable, and the Prince Palatine, he had obeyed and had been received by Queen Mary at Perth on 5 May 1564.

He had not intended to remain in Scotland but Mary's charm had won him over.

> She was so affable, so gracious and discreet, that she won great estimation and the hearts of many both in England and Scotland and mine among the rest, so that I thought her more worthy to be served for little profit than any other prince in Europe for great advantage. I was vanquished and won to tarry with her, and to lay aside all other profits or preferment in France and other countries, albeit for the time I had no heritage but my service. So about two or three months after my home-coming I was sent to the Queen of England, with instructions out of the Queen's own mouth.[2]

Despite Sir James' claims that he worked for virtually nothing, Queen Mary did give him a pension and made him her special envoy and a member of her household. Later, in his memoirs, he was to describe how:

> When Matthew, Earl of Lennox, came to Scotland, before the marriage of his son Darnley with the Queen, I went to the Earl, who told me that his long absence out of Scotland had made him a stranger in the knowledge of the State; but that my lady, his wife, at his coming fra her, had willed him to take my brother Robert's counsel and mine in all he did, as that of her friends and kinsmen.[3]

---

*   Made Sir Henry Killigrew, he became the English envoy to Scotland

The result of Sir James' petition to the queen was that Matthew was restored to his lands of the Lennox, his titles and good name by proclamation of a herald in the Mercat Cross in Edinburgh on 9 October 1564.

Margaret, meanwhile, left at home, despite being overwhelmed with debts, was stripping herself of jewels to achieve her overpowering ambition for her son. To Mary herself she sent 'a ring with a fair diamond'. Lord Moray got a diamond, the Secretary Liddington [Lethington] a watch set round with diamonds and rubies, and most importantly a ring with a ruby went to Sir Robert Melville, described by Margaret as her brother.[4] Melville, in no doubts whatever over Margaret's intentions, wrote that: 'Lady Lennox was in guid hope, that her son, Lord Darnley, suld be better sped than the Earl of Leicester anent the marriage with Queen Mary. She was a very wise and discreet matron, and had many favorers in England for the time.'[5]

Plainly Sir Robert had heard that both Margaret, now allowed by Queen Elizabeth to enter her presence, and her son Henry were at Queen Elizabeth's court. Their main reason for going there appears to have been that on 6 July 1564, together with the queen herself, Margaret was a godmother at the christening of William Cecil's baby daughter, tactfully named Elizabeth.

Mary Queen of Scots, who claimed that she had agreed to receive Matthew Lennox at Elizabeth's request, was much annoyed when the English queen, at the last moment, revoked her permission to allow both the Lennoxes to leave England. This proved to be because Elizabeth had discovered that they meant to take with them 'a son of theirs ... who is an amiable youth', plainly meaning Henry. Elizabeth, guessing that his parents were aiming for a match with the Scottish queen, when she was planning to marry the queen to her favourite Robert Dudley, was piqued.

So also was Mary, who, losing her temper, wrote an angry letter to Elizabeth accusing her of going back on her word. Then, realising that her taunts were enough to cause a diplomatic incident, she hastily despatched Sir James Melville to Elizabeth's court to smooth things over.

Sir James arrived to find Margaret much in favour with the fickle English queen; so also was Henry. Elizabeth is known to have liked good looking young men, this probably being an added reason why she did not want him to marry her cousin, of whose known attraction for the opposite sex she was certainly jealous.

Henry was thought so wonderful that he was sent to meet the new Spanish ambassador, Don Diego Guzman d' Silva, appointed to succeed his predecessor who had died of the plague. Then Margaret's heart must almost have burst with pride as she watched him, at least a head taller than most of the courtiers, dressed in the magnificence of the royal regalia, carry the sword before Elizabeth on all formal occasions. The climax was reached on 29 September when Henry participated in the ceremony as the queen made Robert Dudley Earl of Leicester.

Sir James Melville, watching, eyes agog, famously noted for posterity all that occurred on this memorable day.

> The queen herself helping to put on his ceremonial, he [Leicester] sitting upon his knees before her, keeping a great gravity and discreet behaviour. But she could not refrain from putting her hand in his neck to tickle him smilingly, the French ambassador and I standing by. Then she asked at me how I liked him. I answered that as he was a worthy subject, so he was happy who had a princess who could discern and reward good service. 'Yet', she said, 'you like better of yonder long lad', pointing towards my Lord Darnley, who, as nearest prince of the blood, did bear the sword of honour that day before her. My answer was that no woman of spirit would make choice of such a man, that was more like a woman than a man; for he was very lusty, beardless and lady-faced. And I had no will that she should think that I liked him, or had any eye or dealing that way, albeit I had a secret charge to deal with his mother, my Lady Lennox, to procure liberty for him to go to Scotland (where his father was already) that he might see the country and convey the earl, his father, back again to England.[6]

Melville soon realised that Queen Elizabeth was determined to liaise with Mary Queen of Scots over her proposed marriage to Leicester. She told him that she had a great desire to meet her and even took him to her bedroom where:

> … she opened a little desk, wherein were divers little pictures wrapt within paper, and their names written with her own hand upon the papers. Upon the first which she took up was written 'my Lords picture'. I held the candle, and pressed to see that picture so named. She was loath to let me see it;

at length my importunity prevailed for a sight thereof [and found it to be the Earl of Leicester's picture]. I desired that I might carry it to carry home to my queen, which she refused, alleging that she had but that one picture of his ... Then she took out the queen's picture, and kissed it, and I kissed her hand, for the great love I saw she bore to my mistress. She showed me also a fair ruby, as great as a tennis ball. I desired that she would either send it, or my Lord of Leiester's [*sic*] picture, as a token unto the queen.[7]

Queen Elizabeth refused to part with the ruby, saying that 'if the queen would follow her counsel' she would in process of time 'get them both, and all she had.' In the meantime, in token of her affection, she sent Queen Mary a diamond, which Melville, after being cross-questioned by Elizabeth about everything concerning Mary, from her height down to her clothes, eventually took back to Scotland.

Melville implies that it was actually Mary Queen of Scots who bribed Elizabeth's ministers to win her permission for Darnley to join his father in Scotland. Certainly, somehow it was done. Surprisingly Queen Elizabeth agreed to Margaret's petition for her son to join his father at the court of Queen Mary early in the new year of 1565.

Henry left London on 3 February. Riding to Yorkshire, he stayed briefly with his mother at Settrington. There she made plain to him that it was duty, both as a good son to his parents and to the country to which rightly they all belonged, to marry the Queen of Scotland, thereby becoming king. It was, as she had told him from childhood, the dynasty for which he was bred. While his father, through descent, had a right to the Scottish throne, she, as the daughter of the King of England's sister, should now be Queen of England had she been given her due. Moreover, the Catholic countries of Europe would support a revolution against the Calvinists who had driven Scotland from the true faith.

Henry had heard it all before, his parent's ambition had been drummed in almost from infancy and as a loyal son, it was his duty to achieve it.

On 3 February, in bitter weather, he said farewell to his mother before riding for Scotland. It is easy to picture Margaret, standing before Settringham House, hugging her cloak around her against the wind blasting across the fens from the North Sea. It must have been with a catch in her throat, heart beating fast, that she watched him ride away, followed by five of his father's armed men wearing the grey Lennox livery. He was so tall and handsome in the saddle. Perhaps her last sight of him was turning to doff his cap to her before disappearing from view. So great were their hopes in the early light of that morning in 1565. Little could either of them have guessed that they would never see each other again.

34

THE BITTER BITE OF TRIUMPH

Henry Darnley rode first to take a look at his old home of Temple Newsam, where he had been so happy as a boy. Then, spurring on across the Border, he reached Scotland in just seven days, a journey that usually took a fortnight over the rough roads. Not surprisingly, considering the weather, he arrived with a bad cold, something not reported to his mother, who, had she known about it, might well have made herself ill with worry. At Holyrood, he was told that his father was with the Earl of Atholl at Dunkeld.

Matthew Lennox, since his return to Scotland, had wasted no time in finding allies against the all-powerful triumvirate of Moray, Argyll and Châtelheraut, united against a possible Catholic marriage for the queen. Amongst those who supported him, in addition to Atholl, were the Earl of Caithness and the Lords Seton, Ruthven and Home.[1] Waiting for letters from his father, Henry was entertained by his uncle, Lord Robert Stewart, the Bishop of Caithness. The Earl of Glencairn came to see him, as did another, more sinister visitor, his cousin Lord Morton, whose sycophantic flattery failed to conceal his aim to achieve the lands and title of Angus, as Henry must well have known.

Told that the court was at Wemyss Castle in Fife, Henry borrowed horses from Queen Elizabeth's ambassador, Thomas Randolph, and crossed the Forth by the Queens' Ferry. Then, riding along the north coast of the firth, he kept up a good speed until, on the cliffs before him, the towering block of the early fifteenth-century castle rose before his eyes.

Striding into an inner court, he knelt before the tall, auburn-haired young woman of 23 who was Mary Queen of Scots. Tapping him on the shoulder, she told him to rise and was surprised to find him taller than herself.

Sir James Melville, there as a witness, described in his journal what occurred.

> Her Majesty took well with him, and said that he was the lustiest and best proportioned long man that she had seen; for he was of a high stature, long and small [finely built], even and erect, from his youth well instructed in all honest and comely exercises.

Having spent five days in Dunkeld, Henry returned to cross the Forth on the same ferry as Mary. Melville continues:

> After he had haunted court some time, he proposed marriage to Her Majesty, which she took in an evil part at first, as that same day she herself told me, and that she had refused a ring which he then offered unto her. I took occasion, as I had begun, to speak in his favour, that their marriage would put out of doubt their title to the succession to the crown of England. I know not how he fell in acquaintance with Riccio [sic], but he also was his great friend at the queen's hand, so that she took ever the longer the better liking of him, and at length determined to marry him.[2]

At home at Settringham, from the letters that Matthew wrote to her almost on a daily basis, Margaret learned that her longed for, much planned project had come off. Henry was to marry Mary Queen of Scots.

But others knew of it as well. Such breathtaking news could hardly escape detection. Elizabeth's spies were riding hard for London with the latest information from Holyrood.

Amongst those who supplied it was Mary Beaton, one of the four Marys who served the queen of the same name. Mary Beaton, daughter of an ancient family in Fife, was the mistress of Thomas Randolph, Queen Elizabeth's ambassador in Scotland. Heartlessly exploited, she gave the secrets of her mistress to the man whom she believed to be in love with her. Through her Elizabeth learned every detail of Mary's intended marriage. Thwarted in her plans to gain control of both her and her throne through Leicester, the English queen did not try to conceal her feelings. She was very angry indeed.

Margaret, writing to Matthew, told him that the queen of England's displeasure against the marriage of Mary and Henry was 'full of affectations'. Her letter, like many of his to her, was probably intercepted. Elizabeth's agents were effective. She saw to them being well paid.

Mary Queen of Scots and Henry Darnley were married in the private chapel at Holyrood on Sunday 29 July 1565. On the next day, Monday the 30th, Mary ordered the heralds to proclaim her husband King Henry. As the words rang out there was silence. Men looked at each other, shuffling their feet in embarrassment in the audience chamber. Then a lone voice cried out 'God save his Grace', and heads were turned to see Matthew Lennox, standing erect, defiant in the honour of his son.

35

THE PRICE PAID
FOR A MARRIAGE

As the wedding festivities continued Mary and Henry feasted and danced with their courtiers through several days and nights while Henry's mother, Margaret, remained forsaken in the Tower.

It had all begun in April, some two months after Henry had ridden off for Scotland. Margaret had been at Settrington, when Queen Elizabeth's messengers had arrived. Summoned to go to London immediately, she was not even given time to make proper arrangements for her younger son Charles, then only a little boy of 9. Queen Elizabeth, in her rage against Henry for marrying the Queen of Scotland without her consent – as was dictated by the law of her father Henry VIII – took revenge on his mother. Once again Elizabeth was to get her own back on the cousin she held responsible for her imprisonment by her sister Mary.

Now, as before, she ordered the property of the Lennoxes to be seized and their household dispersed. Even the young ladies boarding were sent back to their relations elsewhere.

Margaret arrived in London on 22 April to be lodged in her usual apartments in Whitehall Palace under house arrest. Meanwhile, in Scotland, Matthew, with no idea of what was happening, was entrusting his letters to her to the Earl of Bedford, the Governor of Berwick, who sent them on to Cecil, telling him 'it can not be but there is some news therein, you may use your wisdom in delivering or retaining them.'[1] Deprived of her letters, unaware of what was happening in Scotland, Margaret waited in fear and confusion to hear what the queen would do next.

It transpired that she was being held as a hostage. Queen Elizabeth, determined to put an end to the marriage, had ordered the return of both Henry Darnley and his father to England to be held under arrest. The futility of this was all too soon to be proved. Sir Nicholas Throckmorton, in an urgent despatch to Cecil, told him that the marriage of Mary Queen of Scots to Henry Darnley was now a fait accompli. Elizabeth, determined to prove her authority by punishing the only important member of the Lennox family still within her power, gave an immediate order that Margaret be sent to the Tower.

Taken down the Thames by Sir Francis Knollys, the barge passed under London Bridge where the heads of recently executed prisoners, on the ends of pikes, glared down with hideous grimaces from the roof of the stone gatehouse.

Entering the prison by the water gate below St Thomas' Tower, the infamous Traitor's Gate, through which both Anne Boleyn and Catherine Howard had so recently passed to end their lives, Margaret believed that she would share their fate. 'Abandon hope all ye who enter here', the words must have rung in her mind as once more she was led captive into the now horribly familiar fortress. Here, so many, even if not executed or killed by some deadly disease, simply vanished from sight like the two little sons of Edward IV had.

She was lodged, it would seem, as before in part of the residence of the Lieutenant of the Tower, adjacent to the Bell Tower in which Queen Elizabeth herself, as she claimed at Margaret's instigation, had been held in her sister's reign. Three hundred years later, as workmen were making repairs, the names of the servants who were with Margaret were found inscribed on one of the 18ft-thick walls.

Upon the twentieth day of June, in the year of our Lord one thousand, five hundred, three score and five, the Right Honorable Countess of Lennoxe's Grace committed prison to this lodging, for the marriage of her son my Lord Henry Darnley and the Queen of Scotland. Here is their names that do wait upon her noble Grace in this place.

M Elizabeth Husey.

M Jhan Baily

M Elizabeth Chambrlen.

M Robert Portynger

M Edward C. Veyne

Anno Domini 1566[2]

(The letter M signified either Mr, Mrs, or Miss)

Margaret was not forgotten. Much effort was made to set her free. Foremost amongst those who tried to rescue her was her new daughter-in-law, Mary Queen of Scots. Deeply concerned as she saw Henry's distress over the fate of his mother, she sent John Hay, her Master of Requests, to plead with Elizabeth in person.

Whatever Hay said failed to move her. Elizabeth, tyrannical as her father, refused to even countenance a reprieve. Told of this rebuff, Queen Mary then wrote to the young king of France, Charles IX, to beg him to intervene. His letter, pleading for Margaret's release, arrived on 30 June, but Elizabeth remained adamant in her refusal to set Margaret free.

In Scotland, only the Congregationalists were pleased; Randolph reported spitefully that 'Some that have heard of the imprisonment of the Lady Lennox like very well thereof and wish both her husband and son to keep her company. It is no small comfort to those who favour God's word to hear that the Queen's Majesty, Elizabeth, is determined to advance the true religion and to abase the contrary.'[3]

He then gave Cecil the details of a plot to capture both Matthew and Henry and deliver them as prisoners to Lord Bedford, the Governor of Berwick, a scheme that had fallen through.

Margaret was still in prison for her fiftieth birthday, which fell on 5 October 1565.

The only good news she had by then received was that on the queen's orders, her little son Charles, left almost alone in the large empty house at Settringham, was being sent to live with a Norfolk neighbour, Lady Knevet, who had married a Mister Vaughan.

Queen Elizabeth, at least feeling pity for the lonely child, then apparently felt some contrition over the plight of his mother, instructing her

Lord Treasurer to send her winter clothing and bedding, the cost of which, surprisingly, she undertook to pay herself.

The list was substantial.

Two petticoats – the one scarlet, the other of crimson silk.

A gown of black velvet furred with konnye [rabbit]

A nightgown of satin furred with the same.

A round kirtle of black velvet.

A piece of Holland cloth at 3s. 4d. the ell

Sixteen ells of Holland cloth, for kerchers and rails, at 6s. per ell, to make handkerchiefs and chemisettes [chemises.]

A French hood, a cornet or white cap, and a billiment [borders of the cap front, usually in lace or jewels]

Twelve pairs of hose or stockings and six pairs of velvet shoes.

Two pairs of slippers, and two pairs of moyles [mules.]

A rug, a quilt, a pair of fustians [bolsters] and two pairs of sheets.[4]

For furniture she had a dining table, six joint stools, a chair and two covered stools, a side table, a table to brush on, four tablecloths and two dozen napkins, eight platters (plates), eight dishes and saucers, four porringers, a salt cellar, two silver spoons and a drinking cup, a basin, a ewer, and a great basin [a hip bath?] for the chamber.

In addition there were a pair of creepers (double triangles on which to make toast), a fire pan, a pair of tongs, a pair of bellows and snuffers.

Two of her female servants, Mrs Elizabeth Hussey and Mrs Elizabeth Chamberlin, who actually slept in the Tower, were amongst those who carved their names on the wall as did others who were lodged elsewhere. But all had to be clothed and fed and paid wages from money which Margaret was forced to borrow, having no income from her estates. Despite her desperate poverty, her portrait, painted by an unknown artist, which originally belonged to Lord Morton and which now hangs in the City of Leeds Art Galleries, was painted at this time, as is proved by it being dated 1565.

The full-length likeness shows her very much the matron in a thick black damask gown, over which she wears a full-length cloak edged with fur. Round her throat is a ruff of lace, while just a few strands of her still red-gold hair, escape beneath a scallop shaped cap. One hand rests on one of the tables, which Elizabeth allowed her to have, while the other holds a glove. Most touchingly, a little pug dog, companion during her captivity, stands on its hind legs, demanding attention, at her feet.

From Scotland Matthew wrote to her continually, although his letters, usually intercepted, seldom reached the Tower. In one written from his house in Glasgow, he tells her the great news that Queen Mary is expecting Henry's child.

To my wife, my Lady Margaret,

Glasgow, December 19, 1565.

My sweet Madge

After my most hearty commendations. If ye should take unkindly my slowness in writing to you all this while (as I cannot blame you to do), God, and this bearer, our old servant Fowler, can best witness the occasion thereof, it being not a little to my grief now to be debarred, and want the commodity and comfort of intelligence by letters that we were wont [to have] passing between us during our absence … My Madge, we have to give God most hearty thanks for that the King, our son, continues in good health, and the Queen is great with child (God save them all) for which cause we have great cause to rejoice the more.

Yet for my part, I confess I want and find a lack of my chief comfort, which is you; whom I have no cause to forget for any felicity or wealth that I am in, But I trust that will amend. Although I do not doubt that their Majesties forgetteth you not, yet I am still remembering them for your deliverance, to work therein as much as they can, as I doubt not but that their Majesties will; else ere you should tarry there any longer, I shall wish of God I may be with you, our life being safe.

Thus being forced to make no longer letter, for want of time, as this bearer knoweth … I bid mine own sweet Madge most heartily farewell, beseeching Almighty God to preserve you in health and long life, and send us with our children a merry meeting.

From Glasgow the 19th December

Your own Mathiu, and most loving husband.[5]

What Matthew did not say, perhaps he did not want her to know, was that Mary and Henry were quarrelling. Only later was he to admit that, in the previous month of November, Mary had 'suddenly altered' in her affection for their son.[6] Even as he was writing, he must have been only too aware that the situation was deteriorating. Mary's half-brother Moray had rebelled against her marriage. Riding at the head of her army, with Henry beside her, she had defeated him in what became known as 'the Chaseabout Raid'. Moray himself had fled across the Border to Newcastle but Mary soon pardoned Châtelhérault for supporting him. Henry Darnley was furious. The Hamiltons were his family's greatest enemies. Encouraged by his father to assert his rights, he told her that as her husband and superior he forbade her to make similar dispensations.

Mary reacted with rage. By Christmas it had become an open secret that the two were constantly in contention. Soon there was open proof. Mary had promised him joint rule. Now this was revoked. At his investiture at Candlemas at the beginning of February, she refused him the right to bear the royal arms. Further to this she made it clear that the promised crown matrimonial would now never be his. This could only be granted by parliament but Matthew swore to Henry that he could exert enough influence to gain it without her consent.

Meanwhile, ignorant of what was happening in Scotland, Margaret remained in the Tower. Little had changed since her last incarceration thirty years before. Then she had been young, with more resistance to the cold, which, even in summer, was still penetrating thanks to the thickness of the walls. The same rats, or their descendants, squeaked and scuttered within them as she lay, so often sleepless, during long reaches of the night. Eagerly she asked her servants, allowed to leave the Tower to go to the markets to buy food, for any news from outside. Was there any word from Scotland? Had the Scot's queen's child been born?

She spent much time doing accounts, endlessly adding up the costs of the food and drink they needed to exist, which seemed to get more expensive all the time. Otherwise she sewed beautiful, intricate embroidery, stitching until it hurt her eyes in the poor light near the fireplace, where she sat to get a little warmth. Most of her silks were of the bright colours so popular in Tudor times. But amongst them were twists of grey, as she worked in some of her own once lovely hair, now faded by all the worry and sorrow that she had known.

36

'FOR WANT OF GOOD COUNSEL'

Melville, who was there at the time, indicates plainly in his memoirs that Matthew Lennox was a predominant influence behind the murder of Rizzio. Many historians appear to have overlooked the fact that Henry's father, allotted some of the best rooms in Holyrood Palace, was there when the assassination took place. Melville, while not openly accusing him, says that 'he knew of the said design'. Nonetheless, he implies that it was largely under his influence that Henry was so disastrously led astray. 'The King was yet very young, and not well acquainted with the nature of this nation.' [1]

'The Earl of Morton had a crafty head', wrote Melville, 'and had a cousin called George Douglas, natural son to the Earl of Angus, who was father to Dame Margaret Douglas, Countess of Lennox, the king's mother. The said George was continually about the king, as his mother's brother, and put into his head such suspicion against Riccio [*sic*] that the king was won to give his consent over easily to the slaughter of Signor David.'

George Douglas, the half-brother to whom Margaret had given sanctuary at Wressil Castle when Henry was still a little boy, was used as a cat's-paw by Lord Morton, as is proved by Melville's account. 'This the Lords of Morton, Lindsay, Ruthven and others had devised, to become that way masters of the court, and to stop the parliament.'[2]

The reason for cancelling or postponing the parliament was that it was known that revocation was to be made to the Crown of land granted to certain nobles during the queen's minority. Amongst others, the Earl of Morton was earmarked to lose some of his estates.

It had also been put about that Queen Mary had been persuaded into doing this by her uncle the Cardinal of Lorraine, who had recently returned to France from the council of Trent. The cardinal had sent an envoy, Monsieur de Vilamonte, to Scotland with a commission 'to stay the queen in no ways to agree with the Protestant banished lords, because that all Catholic princes were banded to root them out of Europe'. He had caused the King of France to write earnestly to Queen Mary to that effect.[3]

Resentment amongst the men, about to be deprived of land, had reached a crescendo. Blame was focussed on Rizzio, known to be an emissary of Rome.

Henry was young, inexperienced and naturally jealous of his wife's infatuation with what, both to him and his father, was an upstart Italian; he had been all too easily manipulated by George Douglas, who, according to Melville, was always by his side. It was George who 'plucked forth the king's dagger that was behind his back and struck Riccio [sic] first with it, leaving it sticking in him', ensuring that Henry's involvement in the murder could afterwards never be denied. Melville then told how:

> The next morning, being Sunday, I was let forth at the gate, and passing through the outer close, the queen, looking forth from a window, cried unto me to help her. I drew near and asked what lay in my power. She said 'Go to the Provost of Edinburgh, and bid him in my name convene the town with speed and come and relieve me out of these traitor's hands. But run fast,' says she, 'for they will stay you.'[4] Then, most significantly, even as the queen was talking to him, Mr Nisbet, master of the household of the Earl of Lennox, was sent with a company to stay me. [5]

Melville kept his head, telling them 'that he was only going to hear a sermon at St Giles' church, for it was Sunday.'[6] Fortunately, they believed him, and once out of their sight, he ran headlong to find the Provost, who said, again with some significance, that he had already had another order from the king, but that nonetheless 'he would draw the people to the Tolbooth'.*

The Provost had been as good as his word but to no effect, because, so he claimed, most people in Edinburgh 'were so discontent with the present government that they desired a change'. This Melville passed on to the queen, through one of her ladies, who returned to tell him that Mary believed that her half-brother Lord Moray, in exile in Newcastle, had been sent for by those around her. On his arrival Melville was to tell him that he was to have nothing to do with the people she now knew to be her enemies.

Moray did arrive the next day, when Melville gave him the queen's message. Distraught, as she threw herself into his arms and kissed him, she told him that had he only been there she would not have been 'so uncourteously handled', and Melville, incredulous, saw him actually burst into tears. [7]

In the meantime, Henry, suddenly aware of how he had been used, promised to abandon the so-called friends who had threatened the life of his wife and their unborn child. Mary told him to discharge the guard at Holyrood, so that on the following night she and Henry, with an escort, escaped from the palace and rode for Dunbar.

Melville then met them somewhere on the road returning from Dunbar to Haddington. The queen, having thanked him profusely for 'my continual care of her honour and welfare', then unburdened her mind to him of some of her sorrow and fear.

That night in Haddington she subscribed divers remissions for my Lord Moray and his dependers, lamenting unto me the king's folly, ingratitude and misbehaviour and also my Lord of Lennox's part, which I supposed had been pardoned; and I excused the same as best I could, imputing it to his youth, and laid the blame upon George Douglas and others; praying Her Majesty, for many necessary considerations, to remove out of her mind all causes of ill-feeling against him, seeing that she had chosen him herself against the opinion of many, and promised him favour again of new. But I could perceive nothing but a great grudge that she had in her heart. [8]

---

* The town-house, meeting place of the burgh council.

The depth of her resentment was shown by her treatment of Morton and his associates, whom Henry had revealed to her as the instigators of Rizzio's murder. Put to the horn as a traitor, George Morton fled to England together with Ruthven, who was stricken with mortal disease. The castle of Tantallon, held by Morton since the death of Margaret's father, Angus, and the houses of his relations were then seized and stripped by the some of the 5,000 soldiers whom the queen had under her command.

Melville continued to describe how Henry Darnley had demanded to know what had become of Morton and his confederates; Melville had told him that he believed they had fled, whither he did not know. 'As they have brewed,' says he, 'so let them drink.'[9]

Henry, it seems, was unaware that the Douglasses would inevitably find some way to take their revenge. He continued to squabble with Mary, taking offence over trifles such as Moray sending a note to her which he thought should have come to him. Melville, summing up the situation and sensing impending tragedy for Henry, so plainly heading for disaster, did his best to intervene.

I travailed earnestly to help matters betwixt them and was so importunate that I was thought so troublesome that Her Majesty desired my Lord of Moray to reprove me, and charge me not to be so familiar with the king; who went up and down all alone, and few durst bear him company. He was disliked by the queen and all as secretly favoured the late banished lords; so that it was a great pity to see that good young prince cast off, who failed rather for want of good counsel and experience than of evil will. It appeared to be his destiny to like better of flatterers and ill company than plain speakers and good men: which hath been the wreck of many princes, who with good company would have produced worthy effects. [10]

37

BROKEN DOWN
WITH GRIEF

M argaret Lennox had been in prison for twenty months, when, on the afternoon of 19 February 1567, she was told that she had two visitors, Lady William Howard* and Lady Cecil, both intimates of Queen Elizabeth. Hoping, yet hardly daring, to believe that they might be bringing news of her freedom, she anxiously awaited their coming. But at first sight of their black robes and sad faces, she knew that something was seriously wrong.

At first she could hardly believe them. The words did not make sense. Henry and his father were dead, murdered with the connivance of Henry's wife, the Queen of Scotland. Henry had been ill with smallpox, that she already knew. But this, this incomprehensible statement, was something she could not understand.

She sat down, awkwardly, as the ladies, having expressed their sympathy, tactfully turned and left the room. Then, as the full realization of what they had told her became clear in her mind, she collapsed in such a frenzy of weeping that those with her believed they were seeing an onset of palsy, as a stroke was then termed.

---

* Wife of the brother of Charles with whom Margaret had been in love.

So intense was Margaret's grief that Queen Elizabeth was told that she was dying; the queen sent her own physician, Doctor Huick, formerly in attendance on Catherine Parr, together with the Dean of Westminster, to minister to her, both physically and mentally, in the Tower.

Cecil greatly pitied her, writing to Sir Henry Nares, 'I hope her Majesty will have some favourable compassion for the said lady, whom any human nature must needs pity.'

An agonising ten days went by before Cecil was able to tell Margaret that word had come from Scotland that Matthew was still alive. The original report that he had died with their son had been false. He could not possibly have been killed with Henry in Edinburgh, having been in Glasgow at the time. Cecil had probably heard this from Drury, still depute governor of Berwick, who sent him the famous drawing showing the near naked bodies lying in the garden with Ker of Fawdonside, Morton's henchmen, his Douglas men, nearby. Passing on all that he knew of what had happened, from Sir James Melville who had just come from Scotland, he told Margaret that most suspicion was focussed on the Earl of Bothwell but that the queen 'was not well spoken of'. [1]

Confident that Margaret herself was now so convinced that Queen Mary had murdered her son that she would not even attempt to communicate with her any more, Cecil advised Queen Elizabeth that she be released from the Tower.

Before leaving she had to pay for the expenses of both herself and her servants for all the time she had been there. Having done so, she was left even poorer than she had ever been before.

The Marquis of Winchester, Queen Elizabeth's Lord-Treasurer, writing to Cecil, told him that although he greatly pitied her, 'broken down with acute grief and utterly destitute' as she was, he could not help her financially because the rents of the Lennox lands, which had been taken into receivership, were held in York, while the queen's receiver was in London. He actually intended to borrow money for her so that she could at least settle her prison debts, and he urged Cecil to beg Queen Elizabeth to allow her to have her money back.[2]

Subsequently, when at last released from the Tower on 12 March 1567, Margaret was once again sent into the custody of Lady Sackville at Sheen. She remained there until, after Mary Queen of Scots eloped with the Earl of Bothwell, Matthew returned to England and his wife.

38

THE FATHER'S STORY

Matthew returned but it was a different Matthew, a man who, it seemed, she hardly knew. In the three years since she had seen him, his hair had turned white and he walked with the shuffling slowness of old age. It was not only his physical appearance that had changed. His mind was obsessed with hatred to the point where at times he seemed insane.

Before leaving Scotland he is known to have instigated, if not actually organised, a hate campaign. Placards depicting Bothwell were posted up through Edinburgh labelled 'Here is the murderer of the King.' Others read 'Farewell gentle Henry but a vengeance on Mary.'[1] A ghostly figure prowled the town crying that Bothwell had murdered the king, while unearthly voices wailed for vengeance for his death.

Slowly, haltingly, Matthew described all that had happened since, in that last letter, he had told her that Henry was well and Queen Mary, God bless them both, big with child.

Now he barely could speak coherently of the woman, the Jezebel, as he called her, who he was convinced had betrayed their poor innocent lamb to his death.

Piecing together what he told her, she realised that the trouble between Henry and Mary had begun shortly after Matthew had written to her in terms of such happiness. Hurt and increasingly resentful of her refusal to grant him the Crown matrimonial, he had become paranoid in his belief that her new favourite Bothwell was heading a cabal to have him killed. Convinced that they would dispose of him in the same manner as Rizzio, he had, with reason, or so Matthew claimed, refused to attend their son's christening at Stirling Castle. Instead he had ridden off, heading for Glasgow, in their own land of the Lennox, to tell his father what was happening and to ask for his advice

He had only gone a short way, however, when he had been seized with such terrible pain that it was only by gripping the pummel of his saddle that he had not fallen from his horse. It must have been poison, put into his food or drink by his enemies in Stirling, so Matthew was convinced. Carried in a litter to Glasgow, to his father's house near the Cathedral, he had been plainly very ill.

As Henry lay barely conscious with pain and fever, the physicians, unconvinced by Matthew's suspicions, had eventually declared that he had smallpox, their diagnosis accepted when pustules broke out on his body, disfiguring his handsome face. The devoted Taylor had nursed him through-out his critical illness, sleeping on a camp bed by his side.

Matthew, if he actually knew the real source of Henry's illness, may have spared Margaret the misery of knowing that Henry had been suffering from secondary syphilis. Most probably he had contracted it in France, where an epidemic of the disease, rampant in Western Europe, had been raging at the time when he was there.

He had been getting better, and Matthew was convinced of that, when the queen herself had appeared. She had ridden over from Edinburgh, coming by way of Stirling, from where a strong party of Hamiltons had escorted her into the land of their enemy, the Lennoxess.

Defying the risk of contagion, she had sat beside Henry, telling him that if he returned with her to Edinburgh, she would sleep with him again as his wife. She had promised Matthew she would care for him herself, assuring him that just as she had nursed her first husband, the dauphin, now, for Henry, she would do the same.

There had been no denying her. Matthew had pled, in fact beseeched her to let Henry remain with him until the doctors at least said he was well enough to travel. But Mary had been adamant and Matthew could have been arrested as a traitor had he refused her order to release his son into her hands. He had watched them leave – Henry, lying in a horse litter, his face covered by a taffeta mask – with the greatest apprehension.

If only he had known the future. He would have faced both death and torture to save their son. The queen, that temptress, that sweet-tongued, beautiful woman, had lured him back to Edinburgh to have him killed.

He should have known what would happen. As part of the christening celebrations, as was customary, Mary had granted pardons. Influenced by the Earl of Bothwell, who according to Melville 'now ruled all in court' [2], James, Earl of Morton, together with no less than eighty of his accursed Douglasses, was amongst those restored to their lands and titles. Henry's fate had been inevitable. He had shouted out to his killers, recognisable in the light of flares, that they were his own kin. But they had shown no mercy, either to him or Taylor, as they had closed in to murder them in the garden of the house called Kirk o'Fields.

Matthew could hardly bear to tell Margaret that some of her own relations had strangled their helpless son. With the sleeves of his own nightgown, they had brutally choked him to death. How bitterly they reviled at the villainy of the Douglasses, those very men to whom Margaret had given sanctuary after her father had begged her to save them from imprisonment in the Tower.

39

'My Ears have been so Astounded'

Queen Elizabeth, told of what had happened, was herself deeply shocked. Although Henry's brutal death and the subsequent grief to his parents appalled her, it was the scandal of her cousin Queen Mary's behaviour that really shook her to the core. At once a courier was sent off, galloping north on horses, frequently changed, bearing an urgent despatch.

Madam

My ears have been so astounded and my heart so frightened to hear of the horrible and abominable murder of your late husband and my slaughtered cousin, that I have scarcely spirit to write ... I should not do the office of a faithful cousin and friend, if I did not urge you to preserve your honour, rather than look through your fingers at revenge on those who have done you such pleasure, as most people say ...[1]

The Lennoxes remained together in London, presumably at Margaret's apartments in the Palace of Whitehall, as although both were in deepest mourning, they are known to have been frequently at court.

Queen Elizabeth had found a use for them once more. Now they could be witnesses against what appeared to be the guilt of her rival queen in conniving at the murder of her husband. Kneeling before Elizabeth, they poured out their accusations against their former daughter-in-law. Elizabeth, after some deliberation, then agreed to return them their Yorkshire estates.

Early in the New Year of 1569 they reached Settrington, only to find that, as during their previous imprisonments, the robbers had been at work. Matthew, in a letter to Cecil, told him that '… my wife and I am owing the sum of three thousand pounds or more; our cattle and our provisions upon our land sold and dispersed, in a manner, for nothing; our jewels, with plate, already at gage [pawned].' Knowing he must soon go back to Scotland, he begged Cecil to ask the queen for a loan of £1,000.[2]

It was Leicester, not Cecil, who replied. The request for a loan was ignored but he told him to go to the Earl of Winchester, the Lord Treasurer, and tell him that the queen had graciously agreed that he and Margaret should receive the yearly rents of their land, albeit the property was to remain in the hands of the royal receivers.

Leicester then gave them the news that did at least bring them some comfort in such a time of great distress. Henry's son, their grandson, James VI, just a year old, had been crowned king of Scotland.

More important still, his mother, Mary Queen of Scots, was held prisoner on an island in Loch Leven. She had been forced by her brother, the Regent Moray, to sign a deed of abdication; the document, of such enormous political significance, was now in the hands of Queen Elizabeth.

In proof of the queen's favour, the Lennoxes were told that she was granting them the use of Cold Harbour Palace on the Thames. Sometimes known as Cole Harbour, it was one of the ports where coal was landed from barges to be carted into the city. The palace itself was dilapidated, much in need of repair. But after the Tower it meant freedom. At least they were together again. Margaret, however, was far from well. Writing to Cecil, 'Good Maser Sekretory', on 27 January 1567/8, she had already told him:

I am sorry my hap was not to meet you at my last being at Court, and although I was not well in health at that time, I am worse at this present of my old colic, or else I had been in place of my letters, to have spoken with you concerning my lord's great loss and mine in the sale of our goods, and the increase that

174

should have arisen thereof, our grounds also unstored at this time [without stock or crops]. My servant hath told me that ye have perused the Commission and Privy Seals, wherein ye may see such authority from the Prince [Queen Elizabeth]: as for letters, likewise, no mention thereof, but rather to have preserved, save that which wanted not help, and that to be sold, but not under value. I am sure the meaning was such, yet in all these wrongs I offered to take our goods again at the same price as was prased, as ye know and yet would, if we might obtain. Otherwise, of course must be the laws to have our own again, as all subjects doth. I send you a note of the sale of our goods, and as they were prased. Good Master Sekratory, as my trust is in you, show me favour in my reasonable suit, and that her Majesty may understand our wrongs and great loss, and I shall think myself, as I have done always, bound unto you, and thus scribbled in haste, and so ill I doubt ye can not read it without the help of my man, to whom I have read it.

Your assured friend,

Margaret Lennox.

Endorsed by Cecil January 27, 1567.[3]

Margaret signed herself only Lennox because Matthew and Henry between them, at about the time of Rizzio's murder, had made a deal with her nephew James, Earl of Morton, by which they had signed away her lands and title in exchange for his sworn support. The bitterness of the knowledge as to where that had led them now only exacerbated her loathing of the man she felt mostly responsible for leading Henry to his death.

Told by Cecil that Mary Queen of Scots was now in England, the Lennoxes hurried to court to repeat their demands for justice for her involvement in the murder of their son. Kneeling together before Queen Elizabeth, they both begged passionately for vengeance. Elizabeth, noticing that Margaret's face was red and swollen with crying, tried to comfort her but nonetheless told them bluntly that she could not do anything to punish Mary without further proof of her guilt.

This Margaret tried desperately to find. Somehow she got in touch with a man who had been Matthew's servant in Scotland and who had been present at the Battle of Langside where Mary Queen of Scots had been defeated prior to her flight into England. Her informant told her that although the Laird of Riccarton had been suspected of involvement in her son's

40

MEMORIAL FOR A SON

Queen Elizabeth personally ordered the investigation into Henry Darnley's death, which began at York in October 1568. Queen Mary, although the main suspect, was not allowed to appear in person but was represented by John Leslie, the Bishop of Ross, and Lord Herries.

The evidence against her rested largely on the letters in a small silver casket belonging to Bothwell, which had been taken from his servant George Dalgleish after he had been sent to fetch them from Bothwell's room in Edinburgh Castle. Within the casket were eight letters, known thereafter as the 'Casket Letters', together with a sequence of sonnets, addressed to Bothwell, and two contracts of marriage between Mary and himself. The letters were later destroyed by Mary's son, King James VI of Scotland and I of England, therefore only copies remain. Their veracity has long been doubted, but if the 'Long Glasgow Letter', supposedly written by Mary to Bothwell just before she took Darnley from his father's care back to Edinburgh, is genuine, it does prove her complicity in planning his death.

Queen Elizabeth, asked by the Duke of Norfolk if the letters were enough to convict the Queen of Scots as a murderess, prevaricated and then ordered the court to be reconvened at Westminster. When it opened in the Painted Court, on 25 November, both Cecil and Leicester attended. Moray made his accusations before Matthew Lennox began a tirade against his former daughter-in-law, demanding vengeance for the death of his son.

The trial dragged on inconclusively. On 6 December Moray was asked to give more proof of his allegations against his half-sister. He produced the Act of Council of December 1567, which declared that the reason for Mary's imprisonment was her involvement in her husband's death. In addition he referred to *The Book of Articles*, compiled by George Buchanan, adherent of John Knox, as a brief.

The trial eventually ended at Hampton Court on 11 January 1569 without any conclusion being reached. Leaving London, Margaret and Matthew returned to Settrington, as is evident from the letter written on 21 November by Mabel Fortescue, one of the young ladies sent as wards, to Francis Yaxley. 'My Good Governor, After my most hearty recommendations, through your help, I have returned in my lady's most honourable service whom, as yet, I find my very gentle and gracious lady ...'[1]

It must have been at this time that the Lennoxes commissioned the Darnley Memorial Picture, designed as a public announcement to justify revenge on the murderers of their eldest son. The artist remains unknown, but the best engraving by George Vertue hangs in the Goodwood Collection at Goodwood House. The picture depicts the interior of a Roman Catholic chapel, thought to be that at Settrington, wherein, on a catafalque, lies an effigy of Henry in full plate armour, his helmet lying at his feet. Below him, his parents, robed in mourning, pray to the image of Christ for divine punishment on his murderers. Behind them kneels their remaining son Charles and before them a small child wears a crown to intimate that he is Henry's son, James VI. Streamers issue from the mouths of Henry's family, calling for vengeance for his death.

Banners with the royal arms of Scotland and those of both the Lennox and Angus families hang over the cenotaph. Scutcheons surround it bordered with scallop shells, insignia of St James and the order of St Michael. One medallion, on the side of the tomb, shows two assassins carrying the strangled corpse of Henry towards a door below a raised portcullis, while another depicts his body and that of the faithful Taylor in the garden of Kirk-o-Field, lying before the ruined house. Strangely, in the right-hand corner of the picture, is shown the battle at Carberry Hill, in which Henry, already dead, plainly was not involved.

The Lennoxes had not been long at Settrington before word came from Scotland that the Regent Moray had been murdered, shot in the back by James Hamilton of Bothwellhaugh as he rode in a cavalcade through the main street of Linlithgow. The assassination, by a rabid supporter of Queen Mary, was made more dreadful in that the house from the window of which the fatal bullet was fired belonged to John Hamilton, Archbishop of St Andrews, whose connivance in the crime was thus made plain.

Immediately, on receiving this news, the Lennoxes set off once more for London, where they were now so popular with the queen that they stayed at Somerset House, the palace built by Jane Seymour's brother Edward Somerset at the height of the family's fortune. Matthew put forward the idea that he and Margaret, as the child's grandparents, would be the ideal people to bring up the little Scottish king. Queen Elizabeth, delighted with the idea, commissioned him to go to Scotland to fetch him. The Lennoxes travelled back as far as Yorkshire together. At Settringham they parted, and Margaret said farewell to the husband who, unbeknown to her at the time, she was never to see again.

41

REGENT OF SCOTLAND

Five months had passed since the murder of Moray. Scotland was still without a regent. The country, divided between two parties, one supporting the king and the other his mother, the imprisoned queen, was virtually in a state of civil war.

As intermittent fighting continued in the absence of any real authority, the Scottish nobles, in charge of the boy king, on the verge of despair, eventually asked Queen Elizabeth to appoint a new regent. Her choice fell on Matthew Lennox, who thus achieved the ambition which had brought him from France to Scotland thirty-seven years before.

Matthew travelled north with Sir William Drury, the Marshal of Berwick. Reaching the town, he found that the Earl of Sussex, in command of the English army, had just invaded the Merse on the Scottish side of the Border and had taken the castles of Hume and Fastcastle. In retaliation, Lord Hume had joined with the Hamiltons and Queen Mary's party, much to the satisfaction of the English ambassador Randolph, who was intent on prolonging the fighting in Scotland on instruction from the English Council.

Sir James Melville, who met Matthew in Berwick, told him of the state of the country. He made it plain to him that many people, in particular the men of the queen's party, as her adherents were termed, hated him as a traitor, the sworn adherent of Queen Elizabeth, who had sent him to subdue the Scots. Melville advised him specifically not to attempt to take control of the government, as it was likely to cost him his life. In particular, he warned him against the malevolence of Sir William Kirkaldy of the Grange, the Fife laird who, as the late Regent Moray's man, had become governor of Edinburgh Castle.

Nonetheless, ignoring the warning, Matthew pursued his way to Edinburgh, where the town was in the hands of the king's supporters. Here, the castle was held by Kirkcaldy, who – together with Queen Mary's former secretary, Maitland of Lethington, and Hume, amongst others – had declared for the now imprisoned queen.

Initially made lieutenant of the kingdom, Matthew was formally declared regent in the following month of July.

Shortly after her husband's arrival in Edinburgh, Margaret, to her astonishment, received a letter from Mary Queen of Scots. Now held prisoner at Chatsworth in Derbyshire, Mary had heard that Margaret believed her guilty of Henry Darnley's murder. Desperate to deny any involvement she wrote:

Madam

If the wrong and false reports of rebels, enemies well known for traitors to you, and alas! too much trusted of me by your advice, had not so far stirred you against my innocency, and I must say against all kindness, that you have not only, as it were, condemned me wrongfully, but so hated me, as some words and open deeds has testified to all the world, a manifest misliking in you against your own blood, I would not have omitted thus long my duty in writing to you, excusing me of these untrue reports made of me. But hoping, with God's grace and time, to have my innocency known to you, as I trust it is already to most indifferent persons, I thought it best not to trouble you for a time, till such a matter is moved that toucheth us both, which is transporting your little son [grandson] and my only child into this country, to the which, albeit I be never so willing, I would be glad to have your advice therein, as in all other things tending him. I have borne him, and God knows with what danger to him and me both, and of you he is descended. So I mean not to forget my duty to you in showing herein any unkindness to you, how unkindly that ye have ever dealt with me, but will love you as my aunt, and respect you as my moder-in-law. And if ye please to know farther of my mind, in that and all other things betwixt us, my ambassador, the Bishop of Ross shall be ready to confer with you. And so, after my hearty commendations remitting me to my said ambassador, and your better consideration, I commit you to the protection of Almighty God, whom I pray to preserve you and my brother, [Charles] and cause you to know my part better than ye now do.

From Chatsworth, this x of July, 1570.

Your natural good niece and loving daughter.

To my Lady Lennox, my Moder-in-law.[1]

Confused by this affirmation by Queen Mary of any involvement in Henry's death, and uncertain as to how and if she should reply, Margaret sent the letter on to Matthew, asking for his advice. Matthew replied to his 'sweet Madge' telling her not to believe a word of it. He had, so he assured her, absolute proof of Mary's complicity in their son's death, written by her own hand. Also, two men, since executed, had confessed to her involvement with Bothwell in the murder, statements which later proved to be untrue.

Matthew certainly had no doubt whatsoever about Mary's guilt. He wrote to the King of Denmark asking for the whereabouts of Bothwell, who, after spending some time in Orkney, was known to have taken refuge there. Subsequently, he sent Thomas Buchanan, a brother of the author of the *Articles* produced at Queen Mary's trial, to Denmark as his special envoy. Matthew asked that Bothwell be sent back to Scotland for examination. Buchanan's reply from the Danish king was commandeered by the Earl of Morton, then at Elizabeth's court. Having read it himself, and shown it to the English cabinet, he sent an edited copy of the letter 'omitting sic things as we thought not meet to be shown' on to Matthew dated 24 March 1570-1.[2] Matthew then continued to correspond with the Danish king and in some of the replies, which he did receive unopened, there was information which caused animosity between him and Morton.

Margaret, who had many letters from her husband, was probably still in Yorkshire when summoned by Queen Elizabeth to attend her as first lady at Windsor Castle.

From there, on 10 October 1570, she wrote to Cecil, just after one of her husband's couriers had arrived from Scotland with news. Civil war was continuing in the north-east between the king's party, led by Lennox, and the queen's party, headed by Huntly, Argyll in the west, and the Lennoxes' perpetual enemies, the Hamiltons, in the central belt and south-west.

A truce had been reached in September but the situation was still volatile. Most of all Margaret worried over what was happening to her grandson, the 4-year-old James VI.

> I beseech you to remember, next to our Sovereign Lady, that innocent King, that he and her may not be the worse of any treaty,' she wrote to Cecil, 'I assure you I find her Majesty well minded for the preservation of him and those that belongs to him. I travail as I am. God spet [speed] me well and inspire her Majesty's heart to do for her own surety, and then I know who will rest the better. I will not trouble you with longer letter, but sends you my hearty commendations.
>
> From the court at Windsor this x of October.
>
> Your assured friend,
>
> Margaret Lennox.[3]

Plainly Matthew had asked her to send him something, presumably by return with the messenger, for she adds this postscript: 'I pray you, good Master Sekretory, certify my Lord of his request declared to you by this bearer.'

Waiting on the queen in Windsor Castle, Margaret became the confidante of the French Envoy to Scotland, Monsieur de Mothe Fénelon, who inveigled her into trying to persuade Elizabeth to marry Francis, Duke de Alençon. Craftily, he used her anxiety over her grandson as a bribe to further his cause. 'I have entered into some intelligence with the Countess of Lennox', he wrote to Charles IX, continuing thus:

> ... by pretending to promise her much on the part of your Majesty for her infant grandson, James of Scotland, if she and the Earl, her husband, would agree with the Queen of Scots; and I have demonstrated to her that the marriage with Monsieur can not be otherwise than advantageous to her: for if the Queen of England shall ever have children, the said Lady Lennox ought to wish them to be French, because of the perfect union there would always be between them and her grandson; if her Majesty should have no issue, still Monsieur would always be found ready to advance the right of her grandson to this crown, against all the others who are now pretending to it. On this the Countess sent to me, that she entreated your Majesty to take her grandson under your protection, and to believe that her husband was as devoted and

affectionate a servant to the Crown as any of his predecessors had been; that she, on her part, desired the marriage of Monsieur with her mistress more than anything in the world; and that, holding the place nearest to her (as first lady of the blood royal) of any one in this realm, she had already counselled and persuaded her to it with all affection. She has given me all the information on this head that she could, but up to the present hour she could only tell me this. That, by all the appearances she could observe in the Queen, she seemed to be not only well-disposed, but very affectionately inclined to the marriage; and that she generally talked of nothing but Monsieur's virtues and perfections; that she dressed herself better, rejoicing herself, and assuming more of the belle, and more sprightliness on his account; but that she did not communicate much on the subject with her ladies, and seemed as if she reserved it entirely between herself and the Earl of Leicester and Lord Burghley. [4]

42

THE SNIPER'S BULLET

As expected, the truce in Scotland, lasting a bare six months, ended in April 1571. The year had begun well for Matthew Lennox with the capture of the castle of Doune from the garrison holding it for Queen Mary. Then he set his eyes on Dumbarton Castle, 'the fetters of Scotland', guardian of the mouth of the River Clyde and main stronghold of the Lennox, the great area stretching up the west coast from Glasgow to the borders of Argyll. Matthew, who had been born there before it had been handed over to the English during the infancy of Queen Mary, envisaged a revival of the influence of his family once the castle was once more his own.

He may have remembered from playing on the battlements as a child, that certain parts of the curtain wall were left unguarded because it was thought that the steepness of the rock made them impregnable to attack; it is certain that in view of his secret knowledge, he enlisted the aid of a Captain Thomas Crawford who, with a party of picked men, volunteered to try to take the castle by surprise. Waiting for the right moment, as thick mist drifted in from the sea, they scrambled up the near vertical rock, finding toe holds in the masonry and clinging to a sapling rooted in a crack, which proved strong enough to hold their weight. Once over the ramparts, the leaders threw down ropes to their companions, pulling them up to join them until, as the mist lifted, a terrified sentry, yelled out the alarm.

Too late to stop them, he saw men reach one of the batteries and swivel the guns round to fire into the building. Terrified as cannon balls rained death upon them, the garrison surrendered in hope of saving their lives.

Their conquerors could hardly believe their good fortune on discovering that amongst the prisoners taken was no less a person than John Hamilton, Archbishop of St Andrews. John was the half-brother of Arran, who now, through joining the Protestant Lords of the Congregation, had been deprived of his French dukedom of Châterherault. A devoted Catholic and strong supporter of Queen Mary, Hamilton had christened the baby King James in Stirling Castle. Subsequently, however, he had arranged the murder of Moray. Afraid that the English might pardon him, his Scottish captors saw to it, that charged in addition with the slaughter of Darnley, he was promptly hanged at the Mercat Cross in Stirling, an atrocity for which his relations at once started planning to revenge.

With the Hamiltons entrenched in Lanarkshire, Kirkaldy of Grange continued to hold Edinburgh Castle for the queen. In May, warned of the approach of an English army, the town council granted him £200 to strengthen the defences. However, it was now realised that Mary's freedom from detention was not imminent, as had been formerly supposed. Some of the lords of the queen's party deserted him. Most importantly, Argyll, having switched sides, was amongst those who attended the King's Parliament, which assembled in Stirling in August 1571.

It opened on 3 September when, although the regalia was still in Edinburgh Castle, a crown, a sword and sceptre were carried before the small figure that strode out, with a specially made tiny gold coronet on its head, to the throne in the great hall of the castle. Behind him walked his proud grandfather, robed, like the little boy, in velvet and ermine. Much rehearsal had been needed for James to memorise the words he had to say; having done so, he looked up at the roof and seeing the gap left by a missing slate, piped up 'This Parliament has got ane hole in it.'[1]

In modern times, everyone hearing this would probably have doubled up with laughter. But in those days the child's words were taken to be an ill omen. Heads were shaken. This could only be a perfect example of the mouths of babes bringing forth truth. Disaster must lie ahead.

It came just a day later. The Hamiltons were waiting their chance. A party of Queen Mary's supporters, led by Sir Thomas Kerr, the Laird of Ferniehirst near Jedburgh and Kirkcaldy's son-in-law, together with William Scott of Buccleuch, Kirkcaldy's closest friend, had devised a plot to kidnap the king.

Kirkaldy planned to lead the raid himself, but was dissuaded from doing so on the grounds that, in the event of his death or capture, there was no one to replace him as leader of the queen's cause. Nonetheless, afraid of what might happen should those in charge lose control, he gave special instructions to Sir David Spens of Wormeston, a fellow laird in Fife, to make the regent his prisoner 'and wait upon him, to save him from his particular enemies'.[2]

Despite having received Wormeston's sworn word that he would obey these instructions to the letter, Kirkaldy was nonetheless apprehensive when, just after sunset on 3 September, the party of armed men, led by the Earl of Huntly, Lord Claud Hamilton, Sir William Scott of Buccleuch and the lords of Arbroath and Paisley, set out to ride through the night. With mounted men leading spare horses to carry prisoners, they reached Stirling at four o' clock in the morning, just before the first light of dawn.

The night watchmen had just finished their rounds as a man called George Bell led the party of armed men up a narrow passage into the town. Bursting into the streets, shouting 'God and the Queen! A Hamilton! A Hamilton! Remember the Archbishop!', they divided their forces.

A Captain Halkerston was sent to stand at the market cross to prevent houses being damaged while Buccleuch and Ferniehirst's Border men, well practised rievers, stole all the horses from the stables and took them to the town gate called the Nether Port. From there, together with those the troopers had led, they would be used to carry the prisoners back to Edinburgh, their hands roped behind their backs.

In the meanwhile, Captain Halkerston having failed to reach the market cross, the soldiers were plundering the merchants' booths. In the ensuing chaos it was their commanders who actually marshalled the Protestant lords, together with the regent, forced at the point of a sword from their lodgings, down the steep street heading towards the Nether Port. However, once on flat ground, Wormeston, to whom Matthew Lennox had surrendered on the promise that his life would be spared, obedient to his word to Kirkaldy, tried to secure Matthew's safety by mounting him behind him on his horse.

It was now first light. The Earl of Mar, realising what was happening, managed to raise sixteen of his armed guard. Charging down from the Castle, joined by men of the town, they drove off the attackers.

The prisoners were rescued, but in the confusion, a Captain Calder, an expert marksman, took his chance. Matthew, easily recognisable by his height and bearing, sitting astride behind Wormeston, was an easy target. Calder raised his musket and fired.

Matthew fell forward, thrown by the force of the bullet onto his horse's neck, as Wormiston, wounded by the same shot, was dragged from the saddle by the regent's bodyguard, to be hacked to pieces by the mob. Terrified that his assailant would next attack the king, Matthew would not dismount until once more within the courtyard of the castle. Collapsing, he was carried in to the castle, past poor little James, who, having run to the door to find out what was happening, saw his grandfather born past him with blood pouring from his wound. Matthew, aware of him standing there, choking back his groans of pain, muttered to those near enough to hear him, 'If the babe be well, all is well.'[3]

Laid on a bed, his wound was seen to be fatal. The bullet had cut his bowels. He was dying from loss of blood. Told this, he summoned the lords who had just been rescued from Kirkaldy's men. Gathered round him they stood with bowed heads as he told them that it had been their choice, rather than his own ambition, which had made him regent of Scotland, a charge which he had undertaken because he had been assured of their assistance in defending the young king, 'whose protection by duty and nature I could not refuse'. He asked them to choose some worthy person to fill his place, to protect his servants and lastly, as the power of speech was leaving him, he whispered 'I commend to your favour my servants, who have never received benefits at my hands; and desire you to remember my love to my wife, Meg, whom I beseech God to comfort.'[4]

Matthew Lennox, his titles proclaimed by a herald, was buried with great ceremony in the chapel of Stirling Castle. As his coffin was lowered there was silence amongst the company, assembled beneath the vaulted roof.

Elsewhere, in the same building, the screams of a man in torment were muffled by the thickness of the walls. Captain Calder, the captured marksman, was being broken on the wheel. As a scapegoat for the Hamiltons, he suffered the worst of medieval tortures before death brought merciful relief.

43

THE LENNOX JEWEL

It was Queen Elizabeth herself who broke the dreadful truth to Margaret of her husband's death. The queen was at Lees, an estate belonging to Lord Rich, when the news of the murder of Matthew Lennox was brought to her. William Cecil, now Lord Burghley, who was with her, showed his concern for Margaret by promptly writing to Sir Thomas Smith, Clerk of the Council, on 8 December 1571. First describing what had happened, he continued: 'Let Mr Sadler know thereof; but otherwise disperse it not, lest it be not true that he is dead, and I would not knowledge come to Lady Lennox before she shall have it from the Queen's Majesty.'[1]

Margaret is thought to have been living in Islington, at Canonbury House, at the time when Matthew died. Named after the canons of St Bartholemews who built a manor house in the fourteenth century, it had been rebuilt in 1520 before being acquired by Sir John Spencer, together with adjoining land.

The fact that Queen Elizabeth in person told Margaret of what had happened, suggests that she was then attending court. Elizabeth must have tried to console her by telling her that his last words were for her, 'his dear Meg'.

Margaret's own reaction to the brutal death of the husband she had so much loved is not recorded. Known to have been hysterical on word of her son's murder, she may in this instance have collapsed again or else, from sheer strength of character, remained stoic in the public eye. All that is known for certain is that in reaction to both deaths, she set about finding a jeweller who created one of the most beautiful and original memorials to both the husband and the son she had lost.

The Lennox Jewel, eventually bought by Queen Victoria in 1842, is now in the Queen's Gallery in Edinburgh. During what remained of her lifetime, Margaret wore it constantly, either on a ring tied to her girdle or on a chain round her neck.

A heart of gold, enamelled with emblems, it epitomises the depth and constancy of her love for the man thrown by fate in her way. The front of the heart shows the Douglas badge in gems. Two angels, in enamel, support the Scottish crown, made of emeralds and rubies. Below them two others hold a large oval sapphire, emblem of widowhood, while the heart remains symbolic of that of Robert the Bruce, carried by the Black Douglas in a pilgrimage against the Saracens in Spain.

The golden heart opens to show a green wreath surrounding two hearts of red enamel with an inscription 'QUILAT BE RESOLVE', together with a monogram of the letters 'M.S.L.' (Margaret Stuart Lennox) entwined. A death's head in black on a white ground surmounts the words 'DEATH SHALL DISSOLVE'. Two hands clasped and a green hunting horn are above another inscription reading 'QUHA HOPIS STIOL CONSTANTLY WITH PATIENCE SAL OBTEIN VICTORIA IN YAIR PRESENCE', 'who hopes still constantly with patience, shall obtain victory in your presence'.

The reverse side of the jewel shows a red Tudor dragon, a phoenix rising from the flames, a Marguerite daisy and, most poignantly, a pelican feeding its young from its bleeding breast, signifying that Matthew died defending his grandson, the little king. Enclosing these emblems, lettering runs 'MY STAIT TO YOU I MAY COMPARE ZOU QUHA BONTES RAIR', 'my state to yours I may compare, you whose bounty's rare'.

Although large enough to hold a miniature, the locket is empty inside. The shell contains emblems of martyrdom, fire, stakes, a fiend and truth being drawn from a well. A crowned queen sitting on a throne would seem to indicate Mary Queen of Scots, and the inscription 'GAR TEL MY RELEAS', followed by several words made unintelligible by time, suggests that Margaret did eventually believe in Mary's own sworn innocence of involvement in Henry Darnley's death. Most probably this happened after she had been told that Bothwell, under examination, had declared most vehemently that Mary had been totally unaware of the conspiracy to kill her husband on that dark February night at Kirk o' Field.

44

A BOY UNRESTRAINED

Margaret is known to have been still in Islington, at Canonbury House, when she realised that Charles was getting out of hand. This was not altogether surprising: Charles, now 15, had been bereft of both his parents for the greater part of his life. His father had gone to Scotland when he was only 8, leaving Margaret to somehow make a living out of an impoverished Yorkshire estate. Then, by allowing his brother Henry's marriage, without Queen Elizabeth's consent, his mother had been held prisoner in the Tower of London for a period of almost two years.

During that time, left almost alone at Settrington, he must have run wild, making friends with the local lads, who probably taught him to drink, if nothing worse. His father had returned to England only briefly before going back to Scotland on Elizabeth's orders, supposedly to retrieve his young nephew, the little King of Scots. Now, with his father dead and his mother constantly at court, Charles was no doubt trying out the delights of London and making questionable friends.

Margaret, struggling with her own grief and despairing as to what to do with her son, decided to ask Lord Burghley to take him into his household as a ward.

1. Henry VIII – after Hans Holbein the Younger. (National Portrait Gallery)

2. George Douglas, 1st Earl of Morton. (Scottish National Portrait Gallery)

3. Henry Darnley at the age of 9, by Hans Eworth. (Scottish National Portrait Gallery)

4. James VI of Scotland and I of England as a child. (Scottish National Portrait Gallery)

5. *Left*: Queen Elizabeth I, by an unknown continental artist. (National Portrait Gallery)

6. *Right*: Mary I, by an unknown artist. (National Portrait Gallery)

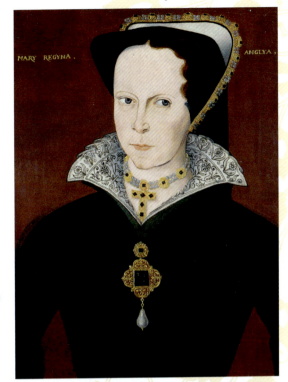

7. *Below*: Lord Darnley and his brother Lord Charles Stuart. (Royal Collection, by kind permission of Her Majesty Queen Elizabeth II)

8. *Below, right*: Lady Margaret Douglas, Countess of Lennox – English School of Portrait Painting in the eighteenth century. (Bridgeman Art Library)

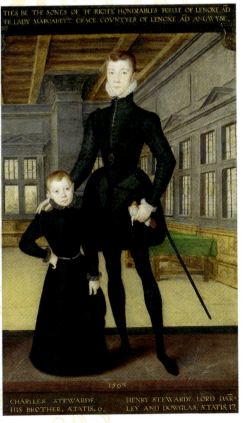

9. The Darnley or Lennox Jewel. (*The Darnley Jewel*, from 'Historical Notes on the Lennox or Darnley Jewel, the Property of the Queen', by Patrick Fraser Tytler (1791–1849), published 1843)

10. Edinburgh Castle. (© Roy Summers)

11. Engraving of Lady Margaret Douglas, 1795. (Bridgeman Art Library)

MARGARET DOWGLAS

COVNTESSE OF LENOX

JAMAIS D'ARRIERE

12. Lady Margaret Douglas painted by Sarah Countess of Essex. (Courtesy of National Galleries, Scotland)

An Original of Mary Queen of Scots. taken at Hardwick, whilst She was in Custody of George Talbot Earl of Shrewsbury Which Queen was Committed to the Keeping of Sr Amias Poulet in 1584, 27 Eliz. two Years before her Tryal after She had been for 17 Years with the said Earl of Shrewsbury and his Countess Elizabeth Daughter and Heir of John Hardwick of Hardwick in Com. Derb. Esq. and the Widow of Sr William Cavendishe

14. Mary Queen of Scots. (© Roy Summers)

3. Linlithgow Palace. (© Roy Summers)

5. Stirling Castle. (© Roy Summers)

16. Tantallon Castle. (© Roy Summers)

17. Temple Newsam House. (Bridgeman Art Library)

18. View of Temple Newsam House around 1750 (oil on canvas) by James Chapman (Fl. 1750). (Bridgeman Art Library)

Islington, Nov.4.1571

My very good Lord

Entering into consideration with myself of the many ways I have approvedly found your Lordship most friendly to me and mine, I could not long delay to bewray [betray] unto you a special grief which long time, but chiefly of late, hath grown up upon me through the bringing up of my only son Charles, whose well-doing and prosperity in all things comely for his calling should be my greatest comfort – so the contrary I could not avoid to be my greatest dolour. And having awakened myself lately, I found that his father's absence so long time in his riper years hath made lack to be in him in divers ways that were answerable in his brother, whose education and bringing up, living only at home with his father and me, at his coming to court I suppose was not misliked of. And though the good hap of this hath not been to have that help of the father's company that his brother had, thereby at these years he is somewhat unfurnished in qualities needful; and I being now a lone widow, am less able to have him well reformed at home than before. Yet the special care that I have that he might be able to continue a worthy memory of his father's house ... hath enforced me for redress to desire your good lordship, above all the pleasures that ever you did me, to accept my said son into your house, to be brought up and instructed as the wards be, so long as shall be needful ... From Islington, this 4 of November, 1571.

Your Lorship's assured loving friend.

Margaret Lennox.

Endorsed –'To my very good Lord, the Lord Burghley, at the Court.'[1]

Lord Burghley's reply to Margaret's appeal was to produce a tutor. Peter Malliet was a Swiss Protestant, a nephew of Huldrych Zwingli, the reformer and confederate of Martin Luther, who, after failing to cut off their food supplies, had been killed in a battle with the Catholic cantons in 1531.

Surprisingly, in view of his antecedents, Malliet fitted in very well with the household by now removed to the house in Hackney, once the property of the Percies, which Henry VIII had granted the Lennoxes shortly after their marriage. From there Peter Malliet wrote to his Swiss cousins, describing his employment.

I have the office of governor and tutor to the young Earl of Lennox, brother of the King of Scots who was murdered, and uncle of the present one. His lordship is a great hindrance to his studies, but induced by the entreaties and promises of the greatest persons in this kingdom, I could not decline but to undertake that burden for a limited time, since I am at full liberty to leave this place whenever I choose. The youth is just entering on his sixteenth year, and gives great promise of hope for the future; for in case the present king, his nephew, should die without lawful issue, he is the sole successor by hereditary right to the Crown of Scotland, and is entitled to be placed at the head of that kingdom and empire. So also, no one is more nearly allied to the royal blood of England, after the death of the present Queen, than his mother, to whom her only son is the heir – although there is now held an assembly, called a parliament, to the end that the undisputed heir may be appointed. What will be the issue I know not. I hear, among other things, the capital punishment of the Queen of Scots has been debated. The Duke of Norfolk has been condemned, and still lies in the Tower.[2]

Malliet was of course referring to the imprisonment of the Duke of Norfolk who, while planning to marry Mary Queen of Scots, had been scheming with an Italian banker called Ridolfi to organise a Catholic rising with the aid of troops from Spain. Norfolk, found to be sending money to Queen Mary's party in Scotland, had been arrested two months previously on 7 September and was now confined to the Tower. Even as Margaret wrote to Burghley, requesting help in controlling her son, Norfolk was being cross-examined, and in January 1552 was tried for high treason. His execution took place in the following June.

In the autumn of that year Queen Elizabeth was thinking of handing over Mary Queen of Scots to the Earl of Mar, who had succeeded Matthew Lennox as regent of Scotland during King James' minority. Mar, however, died on 28 October, reputedly poisoned by Morton, who had entertained him to a banquet in his castle at Dalkeith the previous night. Following this tragedy, Queen Elizabeth, believing it safer to keep the queen in England, abandoned the idea of transferring her to the custody of Morton, now regent in Mar's place.

Her policy, as advised by Cecil, was then to support the young king's party in Scotland, with the result that the leading nobles, headed by Arran, were induced to sign the Pacification of Perth in February 1573.

The Earl of Morton, Margaret's nephew as he was, then occupied the town of Edinburgh where the castle was still held by Kirkcaldy for Queen Mary. Reinforced by an English army commanded by Sir William Drury, and with cannons transported by sea to Leith, the king's party began a bombardment against the ancient walls.

As often happens in early summer in Scotland, there was a period of what Melville called droughty weather. The draw-well dried up, and as the defenders became desperate for water, men were lowered by ropes '... over the walls and rocks of the castle to a well on the west side, which was afterwards poisoned, whereby so many escaped the shot died, and the rest fell deadly sick.'[3]

On 28 May, after eleven days of bombardment, the castle finally surrendered. Sir William Kirkcaldy, Queen Mary's most valiant protagonist, whom King Henry of France called 'one of the most valiant men of our time'[4], was tried and executed for treason; William Maitland of Lethington, Mary's 'Secretary Lethington' upon whose advise she had so much depended on her first arrival in Scotland, died expediently, it is thought by his own hand.

Morton, for all his deviousness and brutality as a man, proved himself competent as governor, his authority being strengthened by the deaths of both Argyll and Arran during ensuing years.

45

CONNIVANCE OF MOTHERS

While the Queen of Scots, abandoned by the government of her own country, remained a prisoner in England in the custody of Lord Shrewsbury, Margaret Lennox, her aunt and mother-in-law, lived quietly in Hackney when not attending Queen Elizabeth at court. The Swiss tutor, Malliet, evidently got her son Charles under control, for nothing is heard of his escapades for the next two years. By that time, however, his mother was seriously considering his marriage; on this important question she was consulting some of her friends, most notably Katherine Duchess of Suffolk, the former Katherine Willoughby, now widowed after marrying the Duke, already by then an old man, when she was only 17.

While at court, Margaret asked Queen Elizabeth for permission to go to Settrington. The queen was immediately suspicious, believing on her spies' information that Margaret was actually trying to arrange a meeting with the Queen of Scotland, with whom she was thought to have been in secret correspondence for some time.

This might have been possible had Margaret wished it so. Mary Queen of Scots was at that moment held prisoner at Chatsworth, in the custody of Earl of Shrewsbury and his wife, the famous Bess of Hardwick.

Permitted a small amount of freedom, she had been allowed to make several visits to Buxton in Derbyshire to take the waters at the famous spa. However, there is no evidence that Margaret even contemplated meeting the queen, who until very recently she had been convinced was involved, if not the main culprit, in the murder of her son.

Whatever Queen Elizabeth suspected about the reasons for Margaret's journey north, the French ambassador de Noailles certainly took it that she meant to rescue her grandson from the clutches of the Scottish nobles before bringing him to England by some means. Writing to his master, King Henry III, on 15 October 1574, he told him that while Margaret was going north to Stirling to visit her little grandson, James VI, he for one believed that she had 'no other purpose than to transfer the little prince into England'.[1]

By the time this dispatch was written, Margaret and her son Charles (now since his father's death the Earl of Lennox), drawn in a carriage by a string of mules, had been travelling for about a week. They had got as far as Huntington, where they stayed with the Dowager Duchess of Suffolk. Here they were met by the redoubtable Lady Shrewsbury, who, with her daughter Elizabeth Cavendish (Sir William Cavendish was the second of Bess' four husbands), had come from her nearby house at Rufford. Nothing would do but they must visit them. All was ready, she assured them. They would be greatly entertained.

Bess had not exaggerated. The house, with all it comforts, so well heated by open fires, was a joy to Margaret whose own finances allowed only the minimum heating in her house. Together with Bess, she sat and gossiped of all the affairs of the court, while, unused to being idle, she stitched at the embroidery at which she had grown so deft.

Outside, in the parkland, Charles and Elizabeth rode together side by side; Charles, plainly attentive to the fair-haired girl with much of her mother's fabled looks, had fallen instantly, and passionately, in love.

Within the house the two dowagers, noting what was taking place, exchanged smiles and knowing looks. From Margaret's point of view it would be a good match. Elizabeth would have money: her mother had accumulated both wealth and property during her vicarious career. For Bess it was also desirable. Should Queen Elizabeth die and also the young king of Scotland, who they said was a frail lad, Charles would be king of both kingdoms through his parent's descent.

There was only one impediment to the union of two young people, so obviously in love. The law of England dictated that Charles, through his royal blood, must have the permission of Queen Elizabeth before he could take a wife. Margaret and Bess, after hasty discussion with the young couple themselves, decided to waste no time. Once the marriage was done they would take the consequences. Queen Elizabeth herself, known to be infatuated with Lord Leicester, would surely look kindly on two young people in love.

There they were much mistaken. Queen Elizabeth did not.

Poor Lord Shrewsbury, overburdened with care and expense in acting as jailer to Mary Queen of Scots, was horrified to find, on coming home to Rufford, that the wedding had just taken place. 'It was dealt with so suddenly, without my knowledge, as I dare insure to your Majesty,' he wrote to Queen Elizabeth, adding in explanation, that 'my wife finding her daughter disappointed in young Barte [Bertie] where she hoped, and as the other young gentleman was inclined to love with a few days acquaintance, she did her best to further her daughter to this match, without having therein other intent than with reverent duty to your Majesty.'[2]

Queen Elizabeth, only hearing of the marriage on 17 November, some three weeks after it had taken place, swore loudly in her rage. Feeling herself duped by two of her ladies-in-waiting, she voiced her anger at them both. On consideration, however, because the Shrewsburys, as guardians of Queen Mary, were useful to her, she decided to defer the punishment of Bess, making Margaret Lennox the scapegoat for all that had clandestinely taken place.

Royal messengers sent to Settringham, which Margaret and the newly married couple had now reached, had to struggle through mud on flooded roads. They bore orders to them all to return to London immediately, a command that Margaret, despite her foreknowledge of what awaited her, had no option but to obey.

46

ONCE MORE IMPRISONED
FOR LOVE

The rain continued, the roads were almost impassable and the mules pulling her carriage, bred as they were to a dry climate, were wretched in the extreme.

Margaret stopped at Huntingdon to rest her exhausted animals, 'both crooked and lame', as she put it, with their 'extreme labour on the way'. She took the opportunity to write to Leicester, enclosing a copy in another to Burghley, written on 3 December, the same day.

To Leicester she described the dangers of the journey which the queen had forced her to make:

The great unquietness and trouble that I have had with passing these dangerous waters, which hath many times forced me to leave my way, which hath been some hindrance unto me … And being forced to stay this present Friday in Huntingdon, somewhat to refresh myself, and my overlaboured moyles, that are both crooked and lame with their extreme labour by the way, I thought good to lay open to your lordship, in these few lines, what I have to [say] for me, touching my going to Rufforth to my lady of Shrewsbury, both being thereunto very earnestly requested, and the place not one mile out of my way. Yea, and as much fairer way, as is well to be proved; and my lady meeting me herself upon the way, I could not refuse it, being near xxx miles from Sheffield.[1]

By this she imputed that rumours of her supposed assignation with Mary Queen of Scots, then imprisoned in Sheffield Castle, one of Shrewsbury's other properties, were untrue. She then told Leicester that while everyone knew she was going to stay with 'my Lady Suffolk', who had been kind enough to escort her as far as Grantham, she was aware that Queen Elizabeth did not approve of the Duchess of Suffolk being at Chatsworth.

> I asked her Majesty, if I were bidden thither, for that had been my wonted way before, if I might go? She prayed me not, lest it should be thought I should agree with the Queen of Scots. And I asked her Majesty, 'if she could think so, for I was made of flesh and blood, and could never forget the murther of my child.' And she said 'Nay, by her faith, she did not think so that ever I should forget it, for if I would I were a devil.'
>
> Now, my Lord, for the hasty marriage of my son after he had entangled himself so that he could have none other, I refer the same to your lordship's good consideration, whether it was not most fitly for me to marry them, he being mine only son and comfort that is left to me. And your lordship can bear me witness how desirous I have been to have had a match for him, other than this. And the Queen's Majesty, much to my comfort, to that end gave me good words at my departure.[2]

From this it can be gathered that Elizabeth herself had a chosen candidate for Charles Lennox to marry. The fact that he had refused to comply with her wishes plainly deepened her resentment against both him and his mother, whom she blamed for encouraging the match. Margaret, pulled by her pathetic mules, eventually reached London and her house in Hackney on 10 December 1574.

The coach was much the worse for the long journey from Yorkshire. The cushions were worn and the family coat of arms painted on the doors almost faded away. Nonetheless, it was hauled out, and the mules, ears laid back in anger, harnessed to it once more. Thus Margaret set off from Hackney, together with Charles and his bride, to Westminster to face Queen Elizabeth's wrath.

On 12 December, in another despatch to Henry III, de Noailles told him that: 'Lady Lennox came this day to Court. She fears greatly the indignation of Queen Elizabeth, her mistress, and that she will send her to the Tower on account of the marriage of her son. Still she relies on friends, who she hopes will save her from this blow.'[3]

The friends, of whom Burghley was the one on whom she most relied, could do nothing to help her. Elizabeth, in her anger, would listen to no appeals. At first the Lennoxes were put under house arrest with orders to speak to no one except those whom the Privy Council permitted.[4]

Christmas, once again, as in that fateful winter of 1561, was to prove an unlucky time for Margaret. On Christmas day, or very shortly afterwards, she was sent once again to the Tower. Resigned to her inevitable imprisonment, she is reported to have said that:

> Thrice have I been cast into prison, not for matters of treason but for matters of love. First when Thomas Howard, son to Thomas, first Duke of Norfolk, was in love with myself; then for the love of 'Henry Darnley my son, to Queen Mary of Scotland; and lastly, for the love of Charles, my younger son, to Elizabeth Cavendish.[5]

Queen Elizabeth, despite the fact that she had initially decided to overlook Lady Shrewsbury's, or Bess of Hardwick's as she is most commonly known, involvement in the clandestine marriage on account of her usefulness as a guardian of Mary Queen of Scots, now, to emphasise her authority, decided that she too must go to the Tower. The two dowagers, if not allowed to meet each other, could certainly converse through their servants; Bess in particular would have had a large retinue, which must have taken up most of the rooms in the building. One of Margaret's servants, a man named John Philips, remained at Hackney to look after Charles, Elizabeth and their baby daughter, Arbella, born as her grandmother remained in prison.

Following their marriage, the young Lennoxes lived with Margaret, having no home of their own. Elizabeth, as the daughter of a rich woman, as Bess of Hardwick had become, should have had money. She was due a dowry of £3,000 from her stepfather, Lord Shrewsbury, but, seizing on the excuse that the marriage had been arranged so secretly, behind his back, he refused to give her anything at all.

The young couple, with their servants, to whom, on the birth of their baby was added a nurse, in addition to Margaret's own household, had to be fed and the latter to some extent paid. The house in winter needed to be heated with a large quantity of coal, and inevitably, as with all old buildings, there were always repairs to be made.

Then to increase Margaret's worries, Charles became extremely ill, coughing continuously from the tuberculosis from which several of his unnamed sisters are believed to have died. This gives a viable reason for why, in the spring of 1577, Margaret was released from the Tower. Queen Elizabeth, for all her known dislike of Margaret, whom she still blamed for her own incarceration so many years before, had felt pity for her when Henry's murder had sent her almost out of her mind. Therefore, it seems probable that told of Charles' fatal illness, she allowed Margaret to be set free before her younger son died.

Charles was still alive in 1577 as is proved by a will made by Mary Queen of Scots, in which she gave the County of Lennox to the Earl of Lennox, held by his late father. In endorsement, she ordered her son, James VI, to facilitate her command as specifically directed.

In her own hand, Queen Mary then added instructions that in the event of the death of her son, she wished the Crown to go to either to Charles, Earl of Lennox, or to Lord Claud Hamilton, 'whichever shall have shown himself most faithful towards herself, and most constantly in his religion'. From this she was implying that Charles could only become King of Scotland if, unlike his father who had become Protestant, he remained true to the Catholic faith.

Queen Mary made her will at Sheffield Manor, a house close to Sheffield Castle, on an unknown date in 1577. Margaret, known to have corresponded with her, sent her a piece of embroidery, some of it stitched with her own hair, now with age and worry turned to grey. Mary, touched by the gift which implied that her mother-in-law was at last convinced that she was innocent of involvement in Darnley's murder, confirmed the longed for confirmation of her birthright.

And I restore to my aunt of Lennox, all the rights that she can pretend to the earldom of Angus, previously to the grant or accord made by my commandment between my said aunt of Lennox and the Earl of Morton, seeing it was then made by the late king my husband and me, on the promise of his faithful assistance if he [Henry Darnley] and me were in danger and required his aid, which promise he broke by his secret understanding with our enemies and rebels that made enterprise against his life, and also took up arms and bore banners against us.[6]

47

My Jewel Arbella

The death of Charles, after all her misfortunes, proved to be almost more than Margaret could stand. She had lost so much, husband, sons and daughters, now all that was left of her once large family were two grandchildren, the young King James of Scotland, whom she was never to see, and the baby girl Arbella, result of that precipitous marriage for which she paid such a price.

With typical determination, she once more faced up to the future. Once again responsibility fell on those shoulders, now hunched with age and rheumatism brought on by long imprisonment within the damp walls of the Tower. She wished only to live quietly, avoiding as much as was possible, all contact with the outside world. But this was not to be.

Margaret had lost the income of the estates in Yorkshire, granted to Matthew by her uncle Henry VIII, which had reverted to male heirs. Her dower lands in the Lennox had been seized by the Scottish Government, headed by her nephew Lord Morton, now regent during the young king's minority. So greatly was she impoverished that she was forced to swallow her pride and borrow from Bess of Hardwick, who, nonetheless, made her pay interest on the loan. Also she had to make repayments on money borrowed from the Crown. Reduced as she was to penury, Margaret somehow struggled on.

Her life was only made happier by the presence of her little granddaughter, Arbella, or Arbell, as she was known. The little fair-haired girl, toddling precariously up and down the stone stairs of the house as she learned to walk, embodied the hopes of her grandmother, for whom she was now all the world. It seems fair to surmise that it was for Arbella, rather than for any personal good will, that Margaret persisted in her correspondence with her erstwhile daughter-in-law, the imprisoned Mary Queen of Scots.

The Lennox title and lands in Scotland now belonged to Arbella, so her grandmother firmly believed. Not so the Scottish government. The Lords of the Congregation, in the name of the young King James, who was still a minor, claimed that Arbella through her English birth had forfeited her right to her inheritance, which was promptly repossessed by the Crown.

Margaret begged Queen Elizabeth to intervene. Putting forward her reasons for doing so, she demanded to know how it was that Scottish law could disregard the legitimate claim. Also, on what grounds could the Scottish regent disinherit the legitimate daughter of Charles Stuart?

Elizabeth, for once, was sympathetic. It cost her nothing to be so. Eager to score one off the Scottish Government, she despatched a courier with a message that 'The Queen finds it very strange that any disposition should be intended of the earldom to the prejudice of the only daughter of the late Earl of Lennox.'[1]

Likewise Mary Queen of Scots, most probably on the supplication of Margaret, and for once in agreement with Elizabeth, added a draft to her will. 'I give to my niece Arbella the Earldom of Lennox, held by her late father; and enjoin my son, as my heir and successor, to obey my will in this particular.'[2]

James, however, disobeyed her. On reaching his majority at the age of 12, he officially bestowed the earldom on his great uncle, Robert Stuart, Bishop of Caithness, who shortly afterwards handed it on to James' cousin, Esmé Stuart, the man of charismatic charm who soon had James in his thrall.

48

POISON?

Arbella was only 4, and still the light of her grandmother's eyes, when on 7 March 1578 no less a person than the queen's favourite, Lord Leicester, came to Hackney to pay them a visit.

Robert Dudley, at the age of 36, thanks to the queen's favour, was now one of the largest landowners in both England and Wales. Dismounting in the court-yard, where weeds sprouted through the stones, he must have been shocked and perhaps saddened to see the state which this great lady, who might have been queen of both England and Scotland, had been reduced. The walls of the house needed pointing, slates were missing and likewise some panes of glass from the windows. The whole building appeared to be in need of repair.

The door creaked open eventually, looking as if it might fall from its hinges as an aged retainer held it wide enough for Leicester to enter into an unlit hall. The house was barely heated, the banister under his hand green with mould.

Following the aged servant, he saw that he still wore the grey uniform of the house of Lennox, now nearly threadbare, the lining having fallen from the coat tails which flapped against his thin shanks. The man looked be nearly starving, judging by the gauntness of his frame.

The stairway ended on a landing from which the servant, standing aside to allow him to enter, opened a door into a long low room. 'Thank you

Fowler', he heard a woman's voice say. The voice was strong but Leicester saw her struggle as she rose from her chair before a fire so small that it gave out hardly any heat. Recognising him, she came slowly forward, the skirts of her long black gown brushing across the floor. She was frail but almost as tall as himself, and her eyes, still blue and piercing, met his unafraid.

It was only as he bowed before her that Leicester became aware of another presence in the room. A little girl was sitting on the floor by the fireplace, playing with a small dog. She looked up laughing, totally nonplussed by this magnificent stranger, who for his part recognised the likeness both to her now dead father and to the grandmother standing before him who had been such a beauty in her day.

It is probable that Leicester came to talk to Margaret about money, sent by Queen Elizabeth, who told of her cousin's destitution at least viewed her situation with concern. All that is known is that he dined with her, and presumably her daughter-in-law, the widowed Elizabeth, perhaps off one of the scraggy chickens that wandered about the place. They were waited on by the man called Fowler who had long been in her employ, though probably now without wages.

Leicester said farewell to Margaret and rode off, leaving her with her little granddaughter, apparently in good health. The two of them, old Fowler behind them, probably standing in the doorway to see him mount, before doffing his velvet cap from the saddle. Then, with his mounted attendants following, he put spurs to his horse and rode away.

Margaret had shown no sign of illness other than the stiffness of her joints, and yet that very night, suddenly and mysteriously, she died. She was sixty-two, an age which in those days was considered to be old.

Inevitably, the suddenness of her death resulted in talk of poison. Suspicion at once fell on Leicester.

According to a common news or scandalmonger, the death of the Countess of Lennox was laid, by popular report, on the Earl of Leicester, who was considered to be so able a poisoner that, if he invited people to dine with him, or invited himself to dine with them, and any one of them died within a month after, he bore the blame of putting a pinch of poison into their food. He had the imputation of poisoning Sir Nicholas Throgmorton, having invited him to dinner, and powdered a salad with poison; likewise of poisoning the Earl of

Essex and M. de Simmiers. He visited the Countess of Lennox at Hackney, and as soon as he was gone she fell into a colic that killed her; and she and all her servants near her were fully of opinion that my Lord Leicester, being there, had procured her dispatch.[1]

So did Leicester kill Margaret as was commonly supposed? Certainly he was known to have disposed of others, including his wife. But if he did kill Margaret by slipping something into her food or drink, what would have been the purpose? How would he, or Queen Elizabeth for that matter, have benefitted from the death of an impecunious, aged lady, whose only possible threat to them could have been that, as a Catholic, she might have been exploited by zealots opposed to religious reform; it seems more likely, in view of the fact that in her letter to Cecil written ten years previously, on 27 January 1558, she had complained of her 'old colic', that she died of some internal complaint. Ironically, it was Queen Elizabeth, with whom she had been at odds for so many years of her life, who, told by Leicester of her destitution, paid for a funeral entirely fitting to a queen. The vault in which Charles Lennox had recently been interred was reopened and Margaret was buried beside him.

Margaret lies in Westminster Abbey, where twenty-five years after her death, an altar tomb was erected by her grandson, then James I of England. Her alabaster effigy, showing her hands raised in prayer, is painted in polychrome and adorned with a golden coronet. Inscribed are details of her lineage, proving her close relationship to the Crown. On the sides of the tomb, her sons kneel as weepers, wearing the full jointed armour of the time. Henry, in ermine lined doublet, has a crown above his head denoting his royal status, while beneath him details of his brief kingship and tragic death are inscribed. On the right-hand side of the foot of the tomb Margaret's lineage is detailed.

This ladye had to her great-grandfather King Edward 4, to her grandfather King Henry 7, to her uncle King Henry 8, to her cousin-german King Edward 6, to her brother King James of Scotland the 5, to her grandchild King James 6. Having to her great-grandmother and grandmother two queens, both named Elizabeth [Elizabeth Woodville and Elizabeth of York] to her mother Margaret, Queen of Scots, to her aunt Mary ye Frenche Queen, to her cousin-germanes Mary and Elizabeth, Queens of England.

On his accession, King James had the bodies of both his parents rein-terred. His mother, Mary Queen of Scots, originally buried in Peterborough Cathedral, was removed to Westminster Abbey. Likewise the body of his father, hastily buried in the Royal Chapel at Holyrood following his murder, was laid in the family vault in Westminster Abbey, as is proved by the main inscription on Margaret's tomb which reads:

Here lyeth the noble ladye Margaret, Countess of Lennox, daughter and sole heir of Archibald Earl of Anguyse, by Margaret Queen of Scotland (her that was eldest daughter to Henry 7th), who beare unto Matthew, Earl of Levenox, her husband, 4 sonnes and 4 daughters. Henry, second sonne to this lady, and father to James IV, now King. This Henry was murdered at the age of 21 years, and is here entombed.

49

DISPUTED INHERITANCE

M argaret died in such poverty that she had virtually nothing to leave. Only the few jewels which had not been either sold or pawned were bequeathed to her little granddaughter, Arbella, when she reached 14. In the event of her dying before that, they were to go to her other grandchild King James VI of Scotland. It would seem that Margaret had sent some jewels to her grandson already, described in the Royal Wardrobe Inventories of his reign.

Received fra my lady Countess of Lennox ane chain of red and enamelled gold, made with little pillars, set with pearls; ane little torquoise; the number of the pearls is fourscore eighteen, and of the cannons of gold twenty-two, and of the little knobs between them twenty-two and enamelled with red, with a tablet and a great pearl hanging thereat, set with diamonds, containing of them twenty-five pieces.

Mair, received of the same lady, a hawk glove set with twelve rubies, and seven garnets, and fifty–two great pearls, and the rest set over with small pearls.

Received also from her ladyship ane ring, set with ane pointed diamond.

Item, another ring, having four sparkles of rubies and a diamond.

Margaret had made Thomas Fowler, the servant and sometimes messenger whom she obviously trusted implicitly, the only executor of her will. From her prison, in the autumn of 1579, Mary Queen of Scots, in her own hand, sent him a warrant authorising him to give the jewels left to Arbella to Bess of Hardwick.

> Be it known that we, Mary, by the grace of God queen of Scotland, do will and
> require Thomas Fowler, sole executor to our dearest mother-in-law and aunt
> … to deliver into the hands of our right beloved cousin Elizabeth, Countess
> of Shrewsbury, all and every such jewel.[1]

Queen Mary's instructions were totally ignored. Thomas Fowler, apparently on the order of King James, instead travelled to Scotland where he claimed he was set upon and robbed. However, as the jewels eventually came into the king's possession, his story may have been an invention to pacify Lady Shrewsbury, indignant as she must have been at her granddaughter being robbed of her rights.

The twenty items in all included 'a jewel set with a fair table diamond, a table ruby and an emerald with a fair great pearl … a clock set in crystal with a wolf of gold upon it … buttons of rock rubies to set on a gown'.[2]

Deprived as she was of her granddaughter's jewels, Lady Shrewsbury used her influence with Queen Elizabeth to make certain that both her widowed daughter Elizabeth and Arbella, her granddaughter, were given pensions; Elizabeth's amounted to £400 annually, while Arbella had only half that sum.

By the autumn of 1578, six months after her grandmother Margaret Lennox had died, Arbella was living with Lady Shrewsbury.[3] Writing to Sir Francis Walsingham from Sheffield, whither she must have gone to supervise the care of Queen Mary, Bess told him that she had 'left my little Arbel at Chatsworth'.

Three years later, in 1581, when Arbella was 7, she spent Christmas at Sheffield with both her widowed mother, Elizabeth, and Bess, her grand-mother. But twelve days later, as the Twelfth Night celebrations were taking place, Elizabeth suddenly collapsed with an undiagnosed illness. Six weeks later, knowing she was dying, she made her will. Bess, her mother, who was with her, testified that 'she did most earnestly sundry times recommend to her Majesty's great goodness and favour that poor infant her only care'.[4]

Elizabeth died, after only seven weeks of illness, on 21 January 1582.* Having left requests to Sir Christopher Hatton, Lord Burghley, Sir Francis Walsingham and Lord Leicester, then the most powerful men at court, to show favour to her 'small orphan', she left Arbella to her mother's custody.

Arbella grew up tied to the apron strings of her formidable grandmother as with ropes of steel. As next in line to her first cousin King James of Scotland, she was used as a political pawn. Several husbands were suggested for her, including Queen Elizabeth's favourite, the Earl of Essex, stepson of the Earl of Leicester, a notorious womaniser who ended his life on the block. An attempt to escape from Hardwick ended in failure; it was only when Queen Elizabeth was dying, in the early spring of 1603, as dissident Roman Catholics tried to kidnap her with the aim of making her queen, that at last she was moved from Hardwick to a house in Kent.

From that time onwards Arbella did have some life of her own. Summoned to the court of King James, she became a lady-in-waiting to Queen Anne. But her troubles were far from over as, almost immediately, Sir Walter Raleigh attempted to raise a rebellion and make her queen. Convicted of treachery, Queen Elizabeth's great adventurer was to spend the next twelve years in the Tower before being released to search again for the fabled land of El Dorado. Failing, he was executed on the old charge of having tried to make Arbella queen. Cleared of all suspicion, in this instance Arbella herself was mercifully spared punishment.

Arbella was already 35 when, without the king's permission, she secretly married William Seymour, grandson of the Earl of Hertford.

James was furious and put William into the Tower while ordering Arbella's house arrest. Both managed to escape, and Arbella even got as far as the French coast before being forcibly taken aboard a warship sent in pursuit. Imprisoned in the Tower, she died there in 1615, by then reputedly insane.

So ended the sad and unproductive life of a girl who, like her Scottish grandmother, had she been more fortunate could have been queen of the two countries, united in 1603.

Arbella Stuart, or Seymour to use her married name, although rumoured to have had a child, did not leave any known descendants. King James VI of Scotland and I of England, on the other hand, is the ancestor

---

* Gregorian Calendar.

of the house of Windsor. Therefore it is through him that the genes of the courageous, formidable and once famously beautiful Margaret Douglas, the grandmother whom he never met, continue in the lineage of the British royal family of today.

Notes

1. The Refugee

1   Strickland, A., *Lives of the Queens of Scotland and English Princesses*, Vol.II, p.125
2   *Ibid.* p.127

3. Wild as a Tantallon Hawk

1   Donaldson.G., *The Edinburgh History of Scotland*, Vol.III, p.35
2   *Ibid.*, Vol.I, p.167
3   *Ibid.*, Vol.II, p.251

4. The Battle for the King

1   *Ibid.*, p.38
2   *Ibid.*, p.40

5. Hunted as an Outlaw

1   State Papers, Vol.IV, p.533
2   *Ibid.*
3   Strangeways to Wolsey, 20 July 1529

7. 'The King's Wicked Intention'

1   Denny, J., *Anne Boleyn*, p.175

8. So Much Destroyed by Death

1   *Ibid.*, p.210

9. 'The Faithfullest Lover that Ever was Born'

1 Statutes of the Realm, Vol.III, p.610
2 *Ibid.*, p.680
3 Statutes of the Realm, Henry VIII, June 1536, pp.680–1

10. Bargaining Counters of the King

1 Cotton MS., Vesp., F. XIII. Holograph.
2 Lord Herbert of Cherbury, Vol.II, p.212 (Perf.Hist)
3 State Paper Office, miscellaneous letters

12. The Flemish Wife

1 Fraser, Lady A., *Six Wives of Henry VIII*, pp.313–4
2 *Ibid.*, p.299

14. The Fall from Grace

1 State Papers, Vol.I, p.692
2 *Ibid.*

15. The Lennox Earldom Restored

1 Donaldson, G., *The Edinburgh History of Scotland*, Vol.3, p.59
2 Privy Purse Expenses of Princess Mary

16. The Price Paid for a Bride

1 Donaldson, G., *The Edinburgh History of Scotland*, Vol.3, p.69
2 Strickland, *Lives of the Queens of Scotland and English Princesses*, pp.238–9
3 *Ibid.*, p.235
4 Strickland, *Lives of the Queens of Scotland and English Princesses*, p.201

17. 'Every Day like Sunday'

1 Fraser, Lady A., *Six Wives of Henry VIII*, p.372

20. The Hostages

1 Strickland quoting Harleian Manuscript etc., p.293

21. 'My Derrest Douchter'

1 State Paper Office, Archibald Earl of Angus to the Countess of Lennox, Edinburgh, 10 June 1548 (date given as that of Gregorian Calendar adopted in Great Britain in 1752)
2 Strickland, *Lives of the Queens of Scotland and English Princess*, pp.300–1
3 State Paper Office, Lennox to Somerset, Scotland, 27 June 1548

22. The Falconer Messengers

1 Strickland, *Lives of the Queens of Scotland and English Princess*, pp.304–5
2 Letter from the Earl of Lennox in Stevenson's *Illustrations of the Reign of Queen Mary*, Maitland Club book. Also Strickland, *Lives of the Queens of Scotland and English Princesses*, p.307

23. The Golden Boy

1 Bingham, C., *Darnley*, p.52
2 Strickland, *Lives of the Queens of Scotland and English Princesses*, pp.310–1
3 State Paper Office, Domestic Records, Northumberland to Cecil. Dated Chelsea.
4 *Ibid.*, dated 7 April 1552

24. 'A Most Victorious and Triumphant Princesse'

1 British Library. Cottonian MS,.Vespasian,F. III. f.378

25. A Conspirator's Smile

1 From John Elder, dated from the City of London, this New Year's day, and the first of the Kalenda of January, 1555, by your humble orator

26. Disputed Inheritance

1 Haynes' Burghley Papers, p.381
2 Unpublished Pieces and Documents relating to the History of Scotland, printed for the Bannatyne Committee, p.278
3 Strickland, *Lives of the Queens of Scotland and English Princesses*, p.322

27. From England's Court to France

1 Forbes Papers, Letter of Sir Nicholas Throckmorton to Queen Elizabeth

28. 'The Great Revenge that Ye might have of your Enemies'

1 Dadler's State Papers, Vol.I, pp.655–6
2 Privy Council to the Duke of Norfolk, January 1559–60

29. Of Soothsayers and Spies

1 Chalmers, G., *Mary Queen of Scots*, founded on a manuscript by Whitaker, J., Manchester historian (London, 1818)
2 Deposition of William Forbes concerning the Lady Lennox, 9 May 1562

30. Arrest

1 State Paper Office MS
2 Endorsed by William Cecil, 'William Forbes contra Lady Lennox', State Papers Office MS

31. 'A Very Wise and Discreet Matron'

1 State Paper Office, Domestic Records
2 State Paper Office, 21 May 1562, see Strickland, *Lives of the Queens of Scotland and English Princesses*, pp.341–2
3 *Ibid.* Domestic, Sheen, 30 May 1562, Strickland, *Lives of the Queens of Scotland and English Princesses*, p.345
4 *Ibid.*
5 *Ibid.*, p.346
6 *Ibid.*, p.347

7   *Ibid.*, p.348
8   *Ibid.*, p.349
9   State Office Paper, Lady Lennox to Cecil, Sheen, 12 August 1562
10 State Paper Office, Lady Lennox to Cecil, Sheen, 22 August 1562
11 Strickland, *Lives of the Queens of Scotland and English Princesses*, p.351

33. A Diarist at Court

1   Bingham, C., *Darnley*, p.84
2   *Memoirs of Sir James Melville of Halhilll*, pp.22–3 (London, The Folio Society,1969)
3   *Ibid.*, September 1564
4   *Ibid.*
5   *Ibid.*
6   *Ibid.*, pp.35–6
7   *Ibid.*, pp.36–7

34. The Bitter Bite of Triumph

1   *Memoirs of Sir James Melville of Halhilll*, p.45
2   *Ibid.*

35. The Price Paid for a Marriage

1   Strickland, *Lives of the Queens of Scotland and English Princesses*, p.359
2   *Ibid.*, p.62
3   *Ibid.*, p.360
4   Strickland, *Lives of the Queens of Scotland and English Princesses*, p.364
5   *Ibid.*, p.363
6   Guy, J., *My Heart is my Own: The Life of Mary Queen of Scots*, p.241

36. 'For Want of Good Counsel'

1   *Memoirs of Sir James Melville of Halhilll*, p.51
2   *Ibid.*
3   *Ibid.*, p.50
4   *Ibid.*, p.52
5   *Ibid.*
6   *Ibid.*
7   *Ibid.*
8   *Memoirs of Sir James Melville of Halhilll*, pp.53–4
9   *Ibid.*, p.54
10 *Ibid.*

37. Broken Down with Grief

1   *Ibid.* p.62
2   State Paper Office MS, Domestic

38. The Father's Story

1   Guy, J., *My Heart is my Own: The Life of Mary Queen of Scots*, p.309
2   *Memoirs of Sir James Melville of Halhilll*, p.62

39. 'My Ears have been so Astounded'

1 Queen Elizabeth to Mary Queen of Scots, 24 February 1567, Calendar of State Papers (Scottish), Vol.2, p.316
2 State Paper Office MS, domestic, Letter from Lennox to Cecil, July 1 1557
3 Strickland, *Lives of the Queens of Scotland and English Princesses*, p.374
4 *Ibid.*, p.376

40. Memorial for a Son

1 Strickland, *Lives of the Queens of Scotland and English Princesses*, p.376

41. Regent of Scotland

1 Robertson's Dissertation, *History of Scotland*, Vol.2
2 Strickland, *Lives of the Queens of Scotland and English Princesses*, p.382
3 *Ibid.*, p.379
4 William Cecil was created Lord Burghley by Queen Elizabeth on 25 February 1571. Dépêche de la Motte Fénélon, Vol.IV, p.84

42. The Sniper's Bullet

1 Spotiswood's Ecclesiastical History
2 Bingham, C., *The Making of a King*, p.58
3 Strickland, *Lives of the Queens of Scotland and English Princesses*, p.383
4 *Ibid.*, pp.383–4

43. The Lennox Jewel

1 *Ibid.*

44. A Boy Unrestrained

1 *Ibid.*, pp.397–8
2 Zurich Letters, second series, Parker Society, pp.200–2
3 Melville, p.101
4 *Memoirs of Sir James Melville of Halhilll*, p.27

45. Connivance of Mothers

1 Dispatch of La Mothe Fénelon to King Henry III of France, 15 October 1574
2 Strickland, *Lives of the Queens of Scotland and English Princesses*, pp.390–1

46. Once More Imprisoned for Love

1 State Papers MS. Margaret Lennox to the Earl of Leicester.
2 *Ibid.*
3 La Mothe Fénélon to Henry III, 12 December 1574
4 *Ibid.*
5 Strickland, *Lives of the Queens of Scotland and English Princesses*, pp. 394–5
6 Document in Cotton. Library, British Museum.

47. My Jewel Arbella

1 Gristwood, S., *Arbella, England's Lost Queen*, pp.26–7
2 *Ibid.*, p.27

48. Poison?

1 Strickland, *Lives of the Queens of Scotland and English Princesses*, quoting *Philipp's Commemoration*, p.398

49. Disputed Inheritance

1 Gristwood, S., *Arbella, England's Lost Queen*, p.30
2 *Ibid.*
3 *Ibid.*
4 *Ibid.*, p.31

BIBLIOGRAPHY

Manuscript Sources, British Library and Museum

Black Letter Tract, British Museum (London, John Charlewood, 1678)

Forbes Papers, Public Record Office SP/1223 MNo.14; deposition of William Forbes

Haynes Burghley Papers, 1562. A Collection of State Papers Relating to Affairs in the reigns of King Henry VIII, King Edward VI, Queen Mary and Queen Elizabeth, left by William, Lord Cecil

Historical Letters, edited by Sir Henry Ellis, 2nd series, Vol. II, The British Museum (Harding, Triphook and Lepard, 1824)

Philips, J., A Commemoration of the Lady Margrit Douglasis Good Grace (London, John Charlewood, printer to the Earl of Arundel, 1578)

Sadler's State Papers, The State Papers and Letters of Sir Ralph Sadler, Knight-Bankeret. Edited by Arthur Clifford Esq. (Edinburgh, Archibald Constable and Co., 1802)

State Papers, Vol.V (published by royal commission)

State Papers, Vols IV and V (printed by commission, Scottish Correspondence)

Statutes of the Realm, Vol.III

Privy Purse Expenses of Princess Mary. Afterwards Queen Mary – A Memoir of the Princess and Notes by Frederick Madden Esq. F.S.A., assistant keeper of the mss. in the British Museum (London, William Pickering, MCXXXiii)

The Cotton MS. Manuscripts collected by Sir Robert Bruce Cotton (1571–1631), British Museum Library

Unpublished Pieces and Documents relating to the History of Scotland, Harleian Manuscript, British Museum (printed for the Bannatyne Committee)

Secondary Sources

Ashdown, D.M., *Tudor Cousins, Rivals for the Throne* (Sutton Publishing Ltd., 2000)

Bingham, C., *Darnley: A Life of Henry Stuart Lord Darnley Consort of Mary Queen of Scots* (London, Constable, 1995)

Bingham, C., *The Making of a King: The Early Years of James VI and I*, (Collins, London, 1968)

Campbell, A., *A History of the Clan Campbell: From the Battle of Flodden to the Restoration Vol 2: From Flodden to the Restoration* (Edinburgh University Press Ltd., 2002)

Chalmers, G., *Mary Queen of Scots*, founded on manuscript by Whitaker, J., Manchester historian (London, J. Murray, 1818)

Denny, J., *Anne Boleyn* (London, Portrait, an imprint of Piatcus Books Ltd., 2004)

Duncan, A.A.M., *Scotland the making of the Kingdom, The Edinburgh History of Scotland, Vol.I* (Edinburgh, Oliver & Boyd, 1975)

Encyclopaedia Britanica, 11th ed. (Cambridge, Cambridge University Press, 1911)

Fraser, Lady A., *The Six Wives of Henry VIII* (London, George Weidenfield and Nicolson Ltd., 1992)

Gristwood, S., *Arbella, England's Lost Queen* (London, Bantam Press, a division of Transworld Publishers, 2003)

Guy, J., *My Heart is My Own: The Life of Mary Queen of Scots* (London, Fourth Estate, 2004)

Lodge, Sir E., *Illustrations of English History*, Vol.I, Chisholm, Hugh, ed. (1911)

Lovell, M.S., *Bess of Hardwick* (London, Little Brown, 2005)

Sir James of Hallhill, *The Memoirs of Melville*, edited by Donaldson, G. (The Folio Society Ltd, 1969)

Myers, A.R., *England in the Later Middle Ages* (London, Penguin Books, 1952)

Nicholson, R., *The Edinburgh History of Scotland: The Later Middle Ages, V.2* (London, Penguin Oliver & Boyd, 1974)

Robertson, W., A Critical Dissertation Concerning the Murder of King Henry, *History of Scotland*, Vol.2 (Cambridge University Press, 1990)

Spottiswood's Ecclesiastical History (Edinburgh, The Spottiswood Society, 1845)

Strickland, A., *Lives of the Queens of Scotland and English Princesses*, Vol.I (Edinburgh and London, William Blackwood & Sons, 1850)

Strickland, A., *Lives of the Queens of Scotland and English Princesses*, Vol.II (Edinburgh and London, William Blackwood & Sons, 1850)

Zurich Letters, second series (pub. for Parker Society by Cambridge University Press, 1842)

INDEX